THE OFFICIAL
MANCHESTER UNITED

ANNUAL 2005

ADAM BOSTOCK

First published in 2004

Manufactured and
distributed by
Carlton Publishing Group
20 Mortimer Street
London W1T 3JW

A CIP catalogue of this book is
available from the British Library.

ISBN 0 23300 099 2

Executive Editor: **Roland Hall**
Project Art Director: **Darren Jordan**
Design: **Andy Jones**
Photography: **John and Matthew Peters/
    Tom Purslow, Manchester United FC**
Picture Research: **Stephen O'Kelly**
Production: **Lisa French**

Printed in Italy

Fans can purchase most of the photos in this
book as prints from: www.manutdpics.com

Contents

Republic of Ireland

Roy Keane (Cork)
Signed from: Nottingham Forest (England)

John O'Shea (Waterford)
Manchester United Academy

Liam Miller (Waterford)
Signed from: Celtic (Scotland)

Scotland

Darren Fletcher (Edinburgh)
Manchester United Academy

United States of America

Tim Howard (Brunswick)
Signed from: NY/NJ Metrostars

Portugal

Cristiano Ronaldo (Madeira)
Signed from: Sporting Lisbon

Brazil

Kleberson (Urai)
Signed from: Atletico Parana

Cameroon

Eric Djemba-Djemba (Douala)
Signed from: FC Nantes (France)

Uruguay

Diego Forlan
(Montevideo)
Signed from: Independiente (Argenti

Manchester United
aim to be the best football
club in the world and to
achieve this, they need to
attract players from all
four corners of the globe.
Here you can see exactly
where Fergie finds his
players, from local to
long-haul destinations…

UNITED

Norway

Ole Gunnar Solskjaer (Kristiansund)
Signed from: Molde

Northern Ireland

Roy Carroll (Enniskillen)
Signed from: Wigan Athletic (England)

Netherlands

Ruud van Nistelrooy (Oss)
Signed from: PSV Eindhoven

England

Wes Brown (Manchester)
Manchester United Academy

Nicky Butt (Manchester)
Manchester United Academy

Paul Scholes (Salford)
Manchester United Academy

Gary Neville (Bury)
Manchester United Academy

Phil Neville (Bury)
Manchester United Academy

Rio Ferdinand (London)
Signed from: Leeds United

China

Dong Fangzhuo (Dalian)
Signed from: Dalian Shide

Alan Smith (Leeds)
Signed from: Leeds United

Wales

Ryan Giggs (Cardiff)
Manchester United Academy

France

Mikael Silvestre (Chambray-les-Tours)
Signed from: Inter Milan (Italy)

Louis Saha (Paris)
Signed from: Fulham (England)

David Bellion (Paris)
Signed from: Sunderland (England)

South Africa

Quinton Fortune (Cape Town)
Signed from: Atletico Madrid (Spain)

August 2003

Manchester United made a fantastic start to the 2003/04 season. It was almost as if they picked up in August from where they had left off in May, when they had lifted the famous trophy for the 8th time in 11 seasons.

Bolton Wanderers were waved aside in the opening match of the campaign at Old Trafford. Fans asked the question, "Who needs David Beckham?" as the new number seven, Ronaldo, tormented the Trotters with his trickery as a second-half substitute. Not to mention the old number 11, Ryan Giggs, curling in the kind of free-kick goal that Becks was famous for – and still is!

If it was all too easy on the opening day at Old Trafford, it was anything but on the second Saturday at St James Park. The Reds had rattled in six goals on their previous trip to Newcastle. This time they had to settle for two, but two were enough to grab all three points. At one point, Sir Alex Ferguson lost his cool and his seat in the dug-out. Incredibly he was sent off, for arguing with the officials! Fortunately Fergie found a TV in Sir Bobby Robson's office, where he watched the rest of the match.

Four days later, the Champions were at home again, where some people expected them to run up a cricket score against newly promoted Wolverhampton Wanderers. But the Midlands club, inspired by Ince and Irwin – the former United stars – did not surrender. They put up a brave fight and had a few good chances to score. These were either spurned, or saved by Tim Howard, while at the other end, the Reds just couldn't build on O'Shea's first goal for the club. It finished 1–0, a disappointing scoreline but a satisfying result. The Reds had now won 7 league games in a row, dating back to April in 2002/03. And their last defeat was a distant memory – Boxing Day 2002, against Middlesbrough!

All good things come to an end. Just when the record books were under threat, the Reds slipped up. And not just with a draw either. Southampton striker James Beattie did what no one expected, and what everyone had failed to do since December, when he scored a winning goal against United in the league. The shock defeat at St Mary's brought to an end what had otherwise been an exciting August.

Above: **Ruud Van Nistelrooy celebrates his first goal of the season.**

Man Utd 4–0 Bolton
16-08-2003 (Giggs 2, Scholes, Van Nistelrooy)
Newcastle 1–2 Man Utd
23-08-2003 (Scholes, Van Nistelrooy)
Man Utd 1–0 Wolves
27-08-2003 (O'Shea)
Southampton 1–0 Man Utd
31–08-2003

REVIEW

Charlton 0–2 Man Utd
13-09-2003 (Van Nistelrooy 2)
Man Utd 0–0 Arsenal
21-09-2003
Leicester 1–4 Man Utd
27-09-2003 (Van Nistelrooy 3, Keane)

Below: **Scholes takes control against Leicester's James Scowcroft.**

Above: **Powell and Ronaldo watch as Ruud scores one of two at Charlton.**

September 2003

Fergie's men had to wait a fortnight to get the frustration out of their system. They did it without too much difficulty, with Ruud van Nistelrooy claiming his first double of the season to see off Charlton Athletic at The Valley. It was just the sort of warm-up that United needed. The following week they faced their biggest challengers, Arsenal, in a game that would surely have a big impact on the championship, even so early on.

United had won nearly all of their crunch games against their three main rivals in 2002/03. They beat Arsenal at home (and drew with them away). They beat Liverpool and Newcastle both at home and away, and were worthy champions. So to lose points at home to the Gunners was a bit of a blow and didn't bode well for the 2003/04 title race. It could have been so different – van Nistelrooy hit the bar instead of the net with his penalty in injury-time. It could have been worse – United didn't lose to Arsenal, although you might have thought it from the way the

Gunners celebrated after the final whistle! In fact, you might have thought they'd won the Premiership, the Champions League… even the World Cup. It was over the top and the FA were not amused. They fined and suspended several Arsenal players including Lauren, Martin Keown and Ashley Cole. Ryan Giggs and Ronaldo were also dragged into it and fined, though it was hard to see why. (OK, so we might be biased, but what do you expect? This is the Man United Annual!)

What the Arsenal game lacked in goals and free-flowing football, the match at Leicester had plenty of. Paul Scholes returned after injury and showed the fans just what they had missed since the middle of August with his brilliant passing and quick thinking. Van Nistelrooy certainly appreciated Paul's presence and, after the misery of missing a penalty against Arsenal, he flattened the Foxes with a fine hat-trick.

October 2003

Above: **Forlan and Scholes watch as Keane scores a header against Leeds.**

United's young players were given their chance to impress in October, as per tradition in the Carling Cup, but also in the Premiership. Darren Fletcher started a league game at Old Trafford for the first time at the tender age of 19 and turned in a solid performance as the Reds beat Birmingham City 3–0. The Scot did most things in 90 minutes except get on the score-sheet. That duty was left to the three old heads of Giggs, Scholes and van Nistelrooy. Ruud set the ball rolling with a penalty after Blues goalkeeper Maik Taylor was sent off for a foul on Scholes, who later scored United's second goal with a terrific shot.

Fletcher kept his place on United's right wing for their next game away to Leeds. This time, he played for the first

hour, by which time the Reds should have been home and dry. Instead, they were thwarted by one of England's best goalkeepers, Paul Robinson, who made some brilliant saves to keep the score at 0–0 until the 81st minute. It was then that Roy Keane climbed above the Leeds defenders to head the ball in from Gary Neville's curling cross. **"One–nil to the Champions,"** sang the away fans. And that's how it finished.

The United line-up looked very different when the Reds returned to

Leeds just 10 days later for a Carling Cup tie (see pages 24–25). But in the meantime, they had more Premiership business to attend to. High-flying Fulham came to Old Trafford and troubled United from as early as the third minute when Lee Clark scored a shock opening goal for the visitors. Fulham should have been further in front before the break but instead they were pegged back by Diego Forlan's equaliser in the dying seconds of the first half. A great time to score, but only if you build on it in the second half. The Reds just couldn't raise their game and Chris Coleman's team took full advantage to score two more goals and record a memorable 3–1 win. Fulham didn't even need Louis Saha to score. His next game at Old Trafford, in January, would see him wearing a United shirt!

Rio Ferdinand feels great after beating his old club, Leeds United.

Man Utd 3–0 Birmingham
04-10-2003 (Scholes, Giggs, Van Nistelrooy)
Leeds 0–1 Man Utd
18-10-2003 (Keane)
Man Utd 1–3 Fulham
25-10-2003 (Forlan)

Above: **Kleberson scores his first United goal against Blackburn.**

November 2003

The Champions started the month in third place; they finished it by playing the team above them, in second place. Chelsea, boosted financially by the billionaire Roman Abramovich, were mounting a serious challenge for the title with expensive new players like ex-United star Juan Sebastian Veron and former Blackburn winger Damien Duff. But it was one of the pre-Roman players who put the knife into United on 30 November – Frank Lampard scored the only goal of the match from

the penalty spot after the ref ruled that Roy Keane had fouled Joe Cole.

It was a cruel end to what had otherwise been a kind month for the Reds. They had recorded three league wins in a row since losing to Fulham in late October.

Portsmouth were pushed aside at Old Trafford, eventually – United needed to send on their star subs, Roy Keane and Ronaldo, to convert their 1–0 lead into a more comfortable 3–0 victory.

United won 2–1 at Anfield, for the second season in a row. Forlan had been United's two-goal hero 12 months before, but this time it was Giggs who delivered a double blow to Liverpool and their Polish goalkeeper, Jerzy Dudek.

Above: **Diego damages Portsmouth.**

Blackburn were beaten, also 2–1, for United's third league win of November. Three points were sealed thanks to the first goal for the club by summer signing Kleberson and the umpteenth of course for Mr Van Nistelrooy. But if the game seemed done and dusted by half-time, with the Reds 2–0 up, it wasn't quite the case. Brett Emerton, who'd earlier watched his native Australia lose the Rugby World Cup Final to England, restored some pride when he pulled a goal back for Blackburn. Some onlookers thought Rovers deserved to go one better and force a draw but happily the Reds held on. Just as well, with the Chelsea defeat just around the corner!

> **Man Utd 3–0 Portsmouth**
> **01-11-2003 (Forlan, Keane, Ronaldo)**
> **Liverpool 1–2 Man Utd**
> **09-11-2003 (Giggs 2)**
> **Man Utd 2–1 Blackburn**
> **22-11-2003 (Kleberson, Van Nistelrooy)**
> **Chelsea 1–0 Man Utd**
> **30-11-2003**

Below: **Van Nistelrooy keeps possession against Liverpool's Steven Gerrard.**

UNITED

December 2003

Above: **Diego scores his first goal and** (left) **his second against Villa.**

Ruud van Nistelrooy went on a goal rush in December 2003. The Dutch star played four league games and netted in three of them, starting with Aston Villa at Old Trafford. First, he fired United ahead in the 16th minute. Then, with fans' thoughts turning to their half-time hot drink or snack, Ruud struck his second goal on the brink of half-time.

There's no better time to score a goal in football – except for the brink of full-time, when Diego Forlan decided to score not just once but twice against Villa! The Uruguayan substitute had replaced Ruud in the 72nd minute but if David O'Leary's overworked defenders breathed a sigh of relief, they were soon sighing in disbelief as Forlan curled a shot into the top corner and then followed up with a neat finish from Kleberson's back-heeled pass. The 4–0 win was United's biggest of the Premiership season so far and didn't bode well for the next visitors to Old Trafford… Manchester City!

City were a banana skin for United in the previous season, as the Reds slipped up both at home (1–1) and away (1–3). But they had no such trouble at Old Trafford in 2003/04 – see page 54 for details.

Ruud continued his scoring spree the following Saturday, away to Spurs. But United's first goal of the game came from a more unusual source, John O'Shea. The Irish defender grabbed only the second goal of his first-team career with a volley from Darren Fletcher's corner in the 15th minute. Eleven minutes later and Ruud made it 2–0 to the Reds with a deflected shot past Kasey Keller in the Spurs goal. Keller's fellow American, Tim Howard, was having a quieter game at the other end but that changed when Poyet scored for Spurs with 27 minutes still to go. It was a tense 27 minutes for United but some solid defending, especially by man of the

match Rio Ferdinand, saw them through to the final whistle with another victory.

The Reds made sure it was a Happy Christmas for their fans when they beat Everton 3–2 on Boxing Day. Butt, Kleberson and Bellion scored for the Champions but the true star was Ronaldo, who terrorised the Toffees with his box of tricks! United didn't even need to bring on Ruud, who watched from the bench.

Ruud was back in the starting line-up for the trip to the Riverside Stadium, but again his goals weren't required to wrap up the win. One shot from Quinton Fortune was enough to beat Middlesbrough and end the year 2003 on a high note for Sir Alex Ferguson, who celebrated his birthday three days later. However, Fergie was fuming at the referee, Mr Messias, who sent off Darren Fletcher for two minor offences.

Man Utd 4–0 Aston Villa
06-12-2003 (Van Nistelrooy 2, Forlan 2)
Man Utd 3–1 Man City
13-12-2003 (Scholes 2, Van Nistelrooy)
Tottenham 1–2 Man Utd
21-12-2003 (O'Shea, Van Nistelrooy)
Man Utd 3–2 Everton
26-12-2003 (Butt, Kleberson, Bellion)
Middlesbro 0–1 Man Utd
28-12-2003 (Fortune)

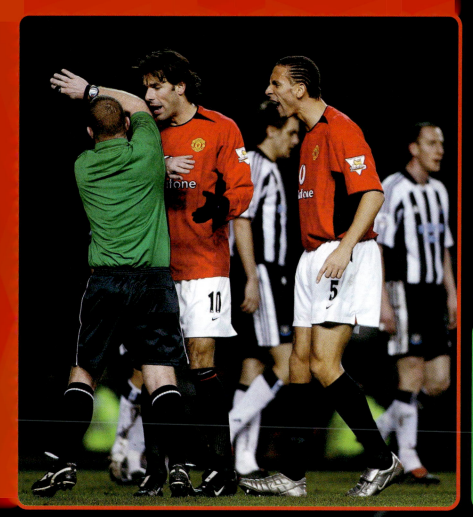

was ruled out by referee Paul Durkin, who said the Frenchman fouled an opponent. Mind you, Newcastle were unlucky as well. They might have had a penalty when Howard tripped Shearer. All's fair in love and football?

The other January match at Old Trafford was a goal feast by comparison. United went 3–0 up and could have scored more against Southampton. Instead they let the Saints slip back into the match with two goals from Phillips. His double strike set up yet another nervy finish for Fergie and the fans, but Howard saved the day when he amazingly tipped over a scissors-kick from ex-United player Higginbotham. Phew!

Bolton 1–2 Man Utd
07-01-2004 (Scholes, Van Nistelrooy)
Man Utd 0–0 Newcastle
11-01-2004
Wolves 1–0 Man Utd
17-01-2004
Man Utd 3–2 Southampton
31-01-2004 (Saha, Scholes, Van Nistelrooy)

Referee Paul Durkin disallows Silvestre's goal against Newcastle.

January 2004

United's first league game of 2004 was on a Wednesday night, away to Bolton Wanderers. This time, there was no red card controversy, just a cracking game of football in which the two goalkeepers played a starring role. Tim Howard was the top man in United's 2–1 win with a performance that Bolton boss Sam Allardyce said was "unbelievable". Sam's talented foreign trio of Okocha, Frandsen and Djorkaeff tried their utmost to beat Tim but in the end only one Englishman – Gary Neville – managed it. Gary unfortunately scored his second own-goal of the season in the 89th minute;

fortunately, his blunder came too late for Bolton to build on it.

United's next away match was not one for the memory banks… unless you happen to be a Wolves fan. So let's keep it brief – Wolves 1 United 0 – and move on.

The Reds played two very different home games in January. First off there was the 0–0 draw with Newcastle. The ball hit the back of the net on one occasion, but Mikael Silvestre's "goal"

Scholes is tackled by Wolves' Paul Butler.

Saha celebrates his first goal for United, against Southampton.

February 2004

It was raining goals for United in February 2004. In fact, their first game of the month was played in every weather condition imaginable! In the first half, there was bright sunshine over Goodison Park when the Reds were leading 3–0 through Louis Saha (2) and Ruud van Nistelrooy. In the second half, there was rain, sleet and snow as Everton staged a courageous comeback to level the match at 3–3. But just when it seemed United had thrown away two points, up popped Ruud at the far post to head in from Cristiano Ronaldo's superb right-wing cross. 4–3 to United! It was a remarkable end to a remarkable match.

Above: **Saha puts United 1–0 up against his old club Fulham.**

While United's attack looked even more formidable with new-boy Saha on board, the defence was starting to rock without Rio Ferdinand. The England defender was now serving his rather harsh eight-month suspension for forgetting a drugs test in September, and the new-look back four was struggling to settle down. If United were fortunate to win at Everton after conceding three goals, they had no such luck at home to Middlesbrough. This time it was United's turn to fall far behind (0–2), fight their way onto level terms (2–2) and then lose to a late goal (2–3), scored in the 80th minute by Job. For the record, Ruud and Ryan Giggs scored for the Reds but it hardly mattered. United were down, but not out of the race just yet.

Leeds, meanwhile, were hoping they wouldn't go down. United's rivals from across the Pennines had been in the bottom three for most of the season but under new manager Eddie Gray, they were

Van Nistelrooy gives Everton's Alan Stubbs a run for his money.

still hopeful of a Houdini-style escape. Hence the never-say-die spirit which saw them draw 1–1 with the Reds at Old Trafford, thanks to Smith's equaliser which came just three minutes after Paul Scholes opened the scoring.

United's defensive difficulties were costing them dear, with Arsenal now seven points clear in the Premiership. The gap widened to nine after the next game, in which Saha scored first against his old club Fulham and ex-Arsenal striker Boa Morte made the final score 1–1 once again. But the game really turned on an incident when Saha was sent flying by Fulham goalie Edwin van der Sar. A penalty for United and a red card for the keeper seemed inevitable – but referee Alan Wiley riled the Reds by taking no action.

Everton 3 – 4 Man Utd
07-02-2004 (Saha 2
Van Nistelrooy 2)
Man Utd 2 – 3 Middlesbrough
11-02-2004 (Van Nistelrooy, Giggs)
Man Utd 1 – 1 Leeds
21-02-2004 (Scholes)
Fulham 1 – 1 Man Utd
28-02-2004 (Saha)

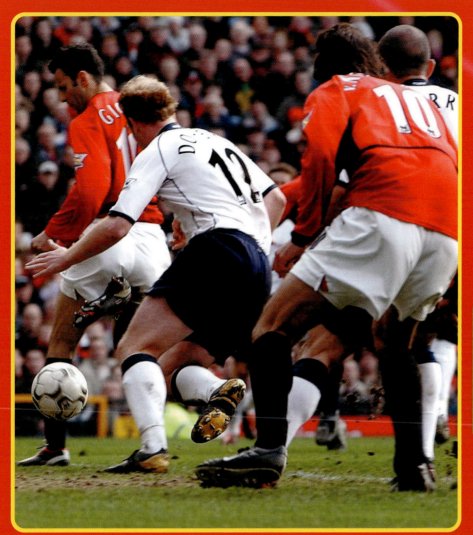

league matches without losing, and were just one win or draw away from setting a new record of 30. United, of course, know a thing or two about breaking records themselves, but they were unable to wreck Arsenal's run. Thierry Henry scored first with a phenomenal shot that swerved round Roy Carroll, substitute Saha equalised for United with just four minutes left on the Highbury clock. Honours were even and tempers were this time kept in check at the final whistle. In some ways full-time felt like half-time – the two teams met again the following weekend in the FA Cup semi-final. See pages 24 and 25 for details.

Man City 4 – 1 Man Utd
14-03-2004 (Scholes)
Man Utd 3 – 0 Tottenham
20-03-2004 (Giggs, Bellion, Ronaldo)
Arsenal 1 – 1 Man Utd
28-03-2004 (Saha)

(Left) **Ryan Giggs flicks in United's first goal and** (below) **congratulates Ronaldo for scoring the third against Spurs.**

March 2004

If February was frustrating, March was mixed – to say the least. In the space of six days, United went from losing by three goals to winning by three goals. Both matches were played locally – the first, a painful 4–1 defeat, took place at the City of Manchester Stadium, the new home of the Blues. For more details of this, please turn to our special feature on Manchester derby matches on pages 54 and 55… if you can bear it!

The second Premiership match in March produced a different performance from United and thankfully a different result! This time, at Old Trafford, they won by three goals, although the second and third goals were not scored until the 90th minute and beyond. Until then, only a cheeky first-half back-heel by Ryan Giggs separated visitors Tottenham Hotspur from the recovering Reds. Bad luck and good goalkeeping from Kasey Keller kept Forlan, van Nistelrooy and Scholes off the scoresheet. Good finishing and fresh legs put the names of Ronaldo and David Bellion on it.

The 3–0 home win over Spurs was just what the doctor ordered, especially as an away game against Arsenal, now 12 points clear, was next on the fixture list. The Gunners had gone through their first 29

April 2004

Saha celebrates his goal against Birmingham City.

If United couldn't stop Arsenal in the league, nobody could. Wenger's men clinched the title with four games to spare, leaving Fergie and Ranieri's teams to wrestle for the runners-up spot. There was a head-to-head on the horizon in May, but before then United had to pick up as many points as possible in April. Easier said than done, especially against a battling team like Birmingham City. The Blues were leading at the break after Grainger had blasted a free-kick past Roy Carroll. The Reds rallied in the second half to win the match with two headers by Louis Saha and substitute Cristiano Ronaldo. Both were set up by Ryan Giggs who, ten years before, was playing in the same United side as Birmingham boss Steve Bruce!

Another of Ryan's former team-mates faced United in the next game – at home to Leicester. Fighting for their Premiership lives, Keith Gillespie and his fellow Foxes foiled the attacking talents of Saha, Scholes and Ronaldo but were undone by a defender. Gary Neville won the match with only his fifth goal in more than 400 appearances… his sixth would follow just a week later!

In fact, Neville nearly scored again just a few days later when his second-half shot was blocked by a Portsmouth defender's arm. But nearly wasn't good enough – United's appeals for a penalty were ignored and so they suffered another shock defeat, built by Stone's first-half strike for the south coast club.

Normal service resumed for the midweek match against Charlton Athletic.

Left: Gary Neville scores United's winner against Leicester.

Gary Neville and Saha scored their second goals of the month to give the Reds a comfortable and much-needed 2–0 win.

However, the winning habit didn't hang around, much to the delight of Liverpool, the next visitors to Old Trafford. After defending stoutly for sixty minutes, the arch-rivals from Anfield pressed forward long enough to snatch a penalty. Three England players were involved – Gary Neville fouled Gerrard and Murphy stepped up to score. It was the third time in three years that he'd scored the winning goal for Liverpool at Old Trafford – definitely a case of third time unlucky for United!

> **Birmingham 1 – 2 Man Utd**
> **10-04-2004 (Saha, Ronaldo)**
> **Man Utd 1 – 0 Leicester**
> **13-04-2004 (G Neville)**
> **Portsmouth 1 – 0 Man Utd**
> **17-04-2004**
> **Man Utd 2 – 0 Charlton**
> **20-04-2004 (Saha, G Neville)**
> **Man Utd 0 – 1 Liverpool**
> **24-04-2004**

Giggs battles with Liverpool's Vladimir Smicer.

May 2004

United's hopes of finishing second were dealt another huge blow by Blackburn Rovers. The Reds lost 1–0 for the third weekend in a row; Blackburn's recent signing, Stead, made the fatal stab with just five minutes to go. To make matters worse, Chelsea won their May Day match 4–0 against Southampton, a result which put them firmly in the driving seat for the following Saturday's showdown at Old Trafford.

Fergie's team was nearly back to full strength for the big game – Ruud returned, after missing almost every game in April. The Dutchman duly delivered United's first goal for three games but this only managed to level the scores after Gronkjaer's impressive opener for Chelsea. The visitors were happy to be level on the day; it meant they finished ahead of the Reds for the first time since the Premiership started in 1993.

The last day of the Premiership campaign saw United make their third visit to Villa Park in 2004. After beating both Aston Villa and Arsenal there in the FA Cup, the Reds completed a hat-trick of victories by conquering the Villans again with two early goals.

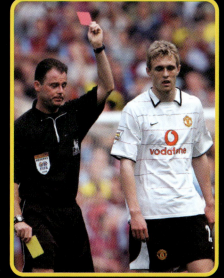

Referee Rob Styles shows Darren Fletcher the red card at Villa Park.

Ronaldo and Ruud struck to make the final score 2–0 after just ten minutes. But the drama didn't end there. Referee Rob Styles made certain of that by booking five players and sending off two – Ronaldo and Darren Fletcher. Fergie fumed after the match but not for long; very soon his focus would switch to the FA Cup Final and beyond to the new season…

Blackburn 1 – 0 Man Utd
01-05-2004
Man Utd 1 – 1 Chelsea
08-05-2004 (Van Nistelrooy)
Aston Villa 0 – 2 Man Utd
15-05-2004 (Van Nistelrooy, Ronaldo)

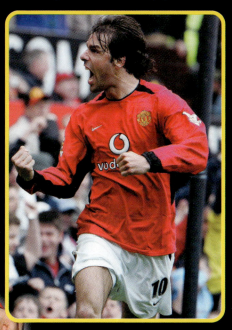

Van Nistelrooy levels the score against Chelsea.

Final League Table 2003/04

Team	P	W	D	L	F	A	GD	Pts
Arsenal	38	26	12	0	73	26	47	90
Chelsea	38	24	7	7	67	30	37	79
Manchester United	38	23	6	9	64	35	29	75
Liverpool	38	16	12	10	55	37	18	60
Newcastle United	38	13	17	8	52	40	12	56
Aston Villa	38	15	11	12	48	44	4	56
Charlton Athletic	38	14	11	13	51	51	0	53
Bolton Wanderers	38	14	11	13	48	56	–8	53
Fulham	38	14	10	14	52	46	6	52
Birmingham City	38	12	14	12	43	48	–5	50
Middlesbrough	38	13	9	16	44	52	–8	48
Southampton	38	12	11	15	44	45	–1	47
Portsmouth	38	12	9	17	47	54	–7	45
Tottenham Hotspur	38	13	6	19	47	57	–10	45
Blackburn Rovers	38	12	8	18	51	59	–8	44
Manchester City	38	9	14	15	55	54	1	41
Everton	38	9	12	17	45	57	–12	39
Leicester City	38	6	15	17	48	65	–17	33
Leeds United	38	8	9	21	40	79	–39	33
Wolves	38	7	12	19	38	77	–39	33

The World Of UNITED
ENGLAND

Gary Neville – Defender
Born: 18 February 1975, Bury

Gary is one of the most experienced footballers in England, having played in more than 60 games for his country and more than 400 for his club. He was the first player from United's famous 1992 youth team to break into the senior national side; he made his international debut on 3 June 1995 when England beat Japan 2–1 at Wembley in a tournament called the Umbro Cup. Gary has since played in one World Cup competition – France

'98 – but he missed the 2002 Finals in Japan & Korea because of an injury. His years of experience and leadership qualities suggest he could one day make a great England captain, if his good friend and former United team-mate David Beckham gives up the job!

Did you know?
Gary Neville will join a small but special group of players if he can help England to win the World Cup before he retires. So far, United legends Sir Bobby Charlton and Nobby Stiles are the only Englishmen who have played in and won both the European Cup Final (1968) and the World Cup Final (1966). United's Champions League success in 1999 puts Gary, Nicky Butt and former Reds star David Beckham on the brink of this remarkable double. Fingers crossed for 2006, lads!

Wes Brown – Defender
Born: 13 October 1979, Manchester

If Gary is one of the most experienced footballers in England, then Wes Brown must be one of the unluckiest! He's battled bravely against ankle and knee injuries, each time bouncing back for more bone-crunching tackles in the service of his club and country. Wes first played for the national team against Hungary on 28 April 1999, towards the end of United's glorious Treble season. Most of his appearances then were at right-back, with Gary Neville sometimes moving into the heart of the defence. Now both Neville and Brown are capable of playing at centre-back or right-back – they're just the kind of player United need at the back when they're fighting for trophies on four fronts.

Did you know?
Wes Brown has been playing with and against England striker Michael

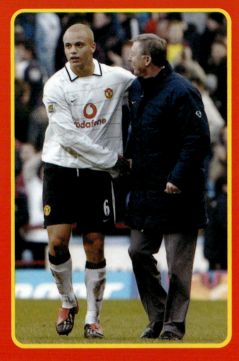

One to Watch

Phillip Bardsley – Defender
Born: 28 June 1985, Salford

Older fans will feel their age when they realise Phillip Bardsley was born the month after United won the FA Cup in 1985 against Everton! Defender Phil has himself tasted cup glory with the Reds, helping the club to win the FA Youth Cup in 2002/03. He also made his first-team debut in a knock-out competition – the Carling Cup, away to West Bromwich Albion on 3 December 2003. Phil played the full 90 minutes and although United went out, losing 0–2, his performance at right-back was described as "outstanding" by Sir Alex Ferguson. The following month saw him come on as a substitute in the 3–0 FA Cup win away to Northampton Town. Look out Gary Neville – the boy Bardsley wants your place in the team!

Owen since the pair were pals at the FA School of Excellence, Lilleshall. Not long after they left Lilleshall, they came face-to-face in an FA Youth Cup match at Anfield – Wes coped well with Owen's pace and United won the match. It was a sign of the many good things to come from the cool and confident centre-back.

Rio Ferdinand – Defender
Born: 7 November 1978, Peckham

Rio Ferdinand was in good company when he first joined United – he found another lad from East London in the dressing room, Mr David Beckham. But Becks moved on at the end of Rio's first season, leaving the former West Ham star with the only southern accent in Sir Alex Ferguson's multi-lingual squad! Not that Rio has had any difficulty in developing an understanding with his fellow United defenders; in his second season, he formed a strong partnership with French star Mikael Silvestre. Only Rio's suspension split them up, much to the delight of opposition strikers who find Ferdinand a tough obstacle to overcome when they play United or England!

Did you know?
Rio played as a striker when he was at junior school, scoring goals for a team called Bloomfields. He was in central midfield when West Ham scouts spotted him at the age of 14… and now he's one of the best centre-backs in the business. Maybe next he'll be in goal?

The World of UNITED
ENGLAND

Nicky Butt – Midfielder
Born: 21 January 1975, Manchester

Nicky Butt's future with Manchester United was in doubt during the 2003/04 season when he requested a transfer and Sir Alex Ferguson agreed – reluctantly – to let him go. It all boiled down to Nicky's desire to start as many matches as possible, partly so he could keep his international career alive. He first played for England on 29 March 1997, helping them to beat Mexico 2–0 at Wembley. He has since earned more than 30 caps, but to stay in the England team, you ideally need to be playing for your club week in, week out. The impressive form of Phil Neville in midfield was making this more difficult for Nicky and he therefore asked to leave. But as the January transfer window came and went without a serious offer, injuries to other United players gave Nicky the chance to reclaim his place in the first team. He seized it with both hands, saying: "It was always going to be difficult for me to leave this club. It's the club I have grown up with."

Above: Butt outruns Aston Villa's Pete Whittingham.
Right: Neville keeps things moving on the training ground.

Did you know?
Nicky Butt helped England to win the European Under-18 Championships in July 1993. He has also played international football at schoolboy level and for the Under-21s. Added to his Champions League exploits with United and his World Cup adventure in Japan, that makes Nicky a very well travelled man!

Phil Neville – Midfielder
Born: 21 January 1977, Bury

Phil Neville's successful transformation from defender to midfielder can only benefit both club and country. For United, he can provide the bite and the drive that we'd otherwise miss as Roy Keane winds down his playing days. For England, he can protect the back four with his defensive prowess, while creative midfielders like David Beckham, Steven Gerrard and Paul Scholes sweep forward to support Owen and co. That sort of role suits Phil down to the ground, he's the unsung hero.

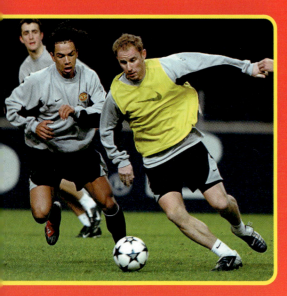

Nicky Butt battles for the ball in training with Kieran Richardson (above) **and Phil Neville** (right).

Not all the time, mind you – he still has a habit of scoring important goals now and again, like the winner away to Rangers in October 2003! Phil's international career may have had its ups and downs, such as missing out on the 1998 World Cup, but with more than 45 caps to his name, he's now one of the most important players in the England squad.

Did you know?
Phil might have played for England at another sport if he'd made a different decision as a talented teenager. Not only was he good at football, he was also keen and capable with a cricket bat. He played for Lancashire's youth team until making the difficult but rewarding choice of football over cricket.

Paul Scholes – Midfielder
Born: 16 November 1974, Salford

Like many other senior players in the team, Paul Scholes was spotted in the shadows of Manchester United and signed up by his local club as a schoolboy. He's since blossomed into a famous player both nationally and internationally. Paul Scholes has scored goals abroad for England in the European Championships and World Cup and for United in the Champions League. But perhaps Paul's favourite score-sheet is from a game he played in his home country, at Wembley Stadium in March 1999. Scholes took the match-ball home after putting three goals past Poland. The following

Paul Scholes goes in search of another vital away goal for United.

season, the England Supporters Club voted him their Player of the Year. Good to know that fans of other teams can appreciate a talent like Paul Scholes! Of course, United supporters worship the turf he treads on, admiring his clever link-play and his knack for scoring crucial goals in the big games. Long may that knack continue!

ENGLAND UNITED

What would the United team look like if radical rule changes forced Fergie to pick English players only?

1. **Tom Heaton**
   Goalkeeper
2. **Gary Neville**
   Right-back
3. **Phil Bardsley**
   Left-back
4. **Wes Brown**
   Centre-back
5. **Rio Ferdinand**
   Centre-back
6. **Chris Eagles**
   Right midfield
7. **Phil Neville**
   Centre midfield
8. **Nicky Butt**
   Centre midfield
9. **Kieran Richardson**
   Left midfield
10. **Paul Scholes**
    Forward
11. **Alan Smith**
    Forward

One to Watch

Alan Smith – Forward
Born: 20 October 1980, Leeds

Fergie's first summer signing in 2004 followed in the footsteps of some famous players by leaving Leeds for United. In the 1970s, defender Gordon McQueen and striker Joe Jordan made the switch from Elland Road to Old Trafford. In 1992, The King – Eric Cantona – did the same and ten years later, Rio Ferdinand became Britain's most expensive player when Manchester United paid £30million to the Yorkshire club.

The World of UNITED

THE UNITED KINGDOM

Wales

Ryan Giggs – Midfield/Attack
Born: 29 November 1973, Cardiff

Probably the most famous Welshman ever to play for Manchester United… just. Ryan has a close rival for that distinction in the shape of Mark Hughes, his international manager

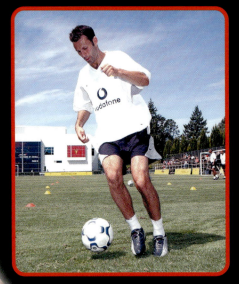

and former team-mate. When Ryan was growing up, dreaming of fame and fortune in football, he idolised Sparky and another goal-scoring hero for the Wales national team, Ian Rush (we forget which club Rush played for… Liver-who?). Nowadays it's Ryan who's scoring and setting up goals for club and country. And perhaps one day he will achieve something that Hughes never managed to do as a player, and represent Wales in a major international tournament. He came so close to it with Euro 2004, losing to Russia in the play-offs. Good luck in reaching Germany 2006, Ryan!

Have United played there?

Yes – quite a few times, and not just in friendlies either. United beat Wrexham, for example, during the early rounds of the 1990/91 European Cup Winners Cup. The away leg was played at the famous Racecourse Ground, just 52 miles from Old Trafford – probably the shortest distance that United will ever travel for a European away match! The other Welsh clubs in the English League, Swansea City and Cardiff City, haven't played against the Reds competitively for many years. But United have been to Cardiff more recently to play in cup finals and in FA Community Shield matches at the impressive Millennium Stadium.

Did you know?

Ryan Giggs once had a swimming pool built at his house; the floor of the pool had the famous Welsh emblem of three feathers painted on it.

Scotland

Darren Fletcher – Midfield
Born: 1 February 1984, Edinburgh

Just what Scottish Manchester United fans, including Sir Alex Ferguson, have waited years for… a Scottish Manchester United player. There used to be so many of them – every United squad that won a trophy between 1957 and 1997 included at least one player born in Scotland. But following Brian McClair's departure in 1998, Scottish players in the home dressing room at Old Trafford became almost as rare as silverware in the Manchester City

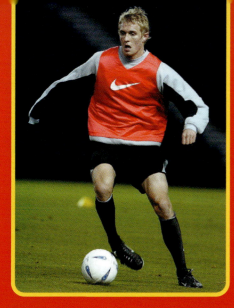

great hero as a young boy wasn't a United player, he played for Arsenal. But we'll forgive you, Roy, because Pat Jennings was one of the greatest British goalkeepers of all time. In fact, he helped the Gunners to win the FA Cup against United in 1979... when Roy Carroll was less than two years old! Jennings also played for Northern Ireland in two World Cup tournaments, in 1982 and 1986. Roy's chances of doing the same don't look particularly promising. The current Northern Ireland squad is very young compared to most international sides and this lack of experience really counted against them in the qualifying group for Euro 2004. Northern Ireland didn't qualify, they finished bottom of their group... without scoring a goal!

Have United played there?
Yes – just as with the Republic of Ireland, the Reds do their best to play a friendly match in Northern Ireland every few years for the many thousands of fans who live there. And if the first team can't make it, the Northern Irish fans can get their United fix by watching the youth team play in the Milk Cup. The Reds won the trophy in 2003, the first time they had done so since 1991.

Did you know?
United and Northern Ireland legend Norman Whiteside became the youngest player to appear in the World Cup Finals in 1982. He was aged 17 years and 41 days, and had barely broken into the first team at Old Trafford. Norm's record was broken during France 98 when a kid called Michael Owen played for England.

UK United

How would the Reds line up if Fergie could only pick players from the four UK countries?

1. Roy Carroll (Northern Ireland)
2. Gary Neville (England)
3. Phillip Bardsley (England)
4. Wes Brown (England)
5. Rio Ferdinand (England)
6. Darren Fletcher (Scotland)
7. Phil Neville (England)
8. Chris Eagles (England)
9. Kieran Richardson (England)
10. Paul Scholes (England)
11. Ryan Giggs (Wales)

trophy cabinet. It's still early days for Fletch, but the promising signs we witnessed during 2003/04 suggest he could nail down a regular place in the United first team.

Have United played there?
Yes – many times, though mainly in friendlies. Scotland has its own league, of course, although there has been talk of its two biggest clubs, Celtic and Rangers, joining the English Premiership. Until that happens, the Glasgow giants will have to make do with facing United in the Champions League. Rangers did so in 2003/04 and probably wish they hadn't because the Reds won both matches, in England and in Scotland.

Did you know?
United were the first English club to win the European Cup in 1968, but they weren't the first British club to do it. Celtic beat the Reds to that honour by one season; they defeated Inter Milan 2–1 in the 1967 final.

Northern Ireland

Roy Carroll – Goalkeeper
Born: 30 September 1977, Enniskillen

The capital city of Northern Ireland – Belfast – was the birthplace of perhaps the greatest Manchester United player ever, George Best. But Roy Carroll's

Above: **Liam Miller signs for the club under the watchful eye of Sir Alex.**

Roy Keane – Midfield
Born: 10 August 1971, Cork

United's inspirational captain may one day be regarded as the best Irish player the club has ever had. But a place in the history books can wait, as Roy is hoping to keep playing for at least another season or three! Keano is certainly one of the most successful Irish players of all time, having won medals virtually every season since joining the Reds from Nottingham Forest in 1993. Forest were his first club in England; previously he played for Cobh Ramblers, a much smaller club in the Irish League.

Did you know?
United's only manager from outside the UK so far, Mr Frank O'Farrell, came from Ireland. Like Liam Miller and Roy

Liam Miller – Midfield
Born: 13 February 1981, Cork

Don't be confused by the fact that Liam joined United from one of Scotland's biggest clubs (Celtic), or the fact that his Scottish manager (Fergie) compared him to a former Scotland striker (Brian McClair). Liam Miller is the latest in a long line of young men from Ireland who have proudly pulled on the red shirt of Manchester United. Other Irishmen who have graced the home dressing room at Old Trafford include legends like Denis Irwin, Paul McGrath, Kevin Moran and Frank Stapleton plus – of course – Liam's current team-mates John O'Shea and Roy Keane. Liam hopes to emulate his heroes one day and represent the Republic of Ireland in a major international tournament like the World Cup. He has already played for his country at Under-21 level, alongside another rising star at United, Paul Tierney.

Have United played there?
Yes – the Reds visit Ireland most years for a friendly match, usually in the summer. For example, in July 2002 they played Shelbourne, who were then the Irish champions. Ruud van Nistelrooy scored a hat-trick in United's 5–0 win but the biggest cheers at Dublin's Tolka Park were for Roy Keane, a national hero in Ireland – especially with the many thousands of United fans living there! There are more than 30 branches of the official supporters club there – about the same number of branches there are in North-West England!

Did you know?
Manchester United have a special partnership agreement in place with Shelbourne. Hopefully this will help the Reds to find the next Roy Keane, Liam Miller or John O'Shea at a young age.

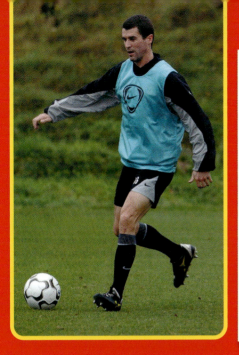

One to Watch

Paul McShane – Defender
Born: 6 January 1986, Wicklow

Promising defender Paul joined United at the age of 16 in July 2002, when he left his school and home in Ireland to follow in the footsteps of John O'Shea. Paul tasted success in his first full season in the Academy, helping the Reds to win the prestigious FA Youth Cup – it was the first time the club had claimed the trophy since Phil Neville was in the youth team, back in 1995. McShane's hard work was noted by Sir Alex Ferguson; the United manager gave him squad number 34 for the Champions League. A great honour, and a sign that McShane's moving in the right direction – even if he didn't get to kick a ball in the first team!

Keane, the former United boss was also born in Cork. O'Farrell took charge at Old Trafford in June 1971 but lasted only until December 1972 when he was sacked after a poor start to his second season.

John O'Shea – Midfield
Born: 30 April 1981, Waterford

Ireland's love affair with Manchester United needed a boost when Denis

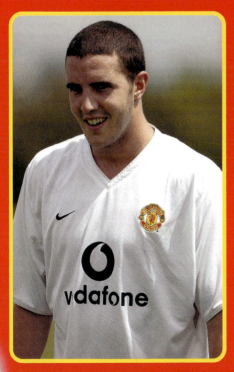

Irwin left the club after 12 years of distinguished service. Then up stepped O'Shea, another Irish defender, to really make a name for himself in the first team. Almost 2 metres tall, Sheasy looks like the perfect candidate to play in the centre of United's defence. But John's speed and skill, not to mention the competition at centre-back from Rio Ferdinand, Wes Brown and Mikael Silvestre, have led to him playing as a left- or right-back. Neither he nor the Irish fans care what position he plays, just as long as he's in the team. Thanks to O'Shea and Miller, the connection between Ireland and Manchester will live on… even when Keano does retire.

Did you know?

John O'Shea's home-town team, Waterford, once played against United in the European Cup, way back in 1968. The Reds were champions of Europe and too strong for the Irish club, winning 3–1 in Ireland and 7–1 back at Old Trafford. Sheasy wasn't around at the time… in fact, he wasn't born for another 13 years!

Cardiff
here we come!

United produced some of their best football of the 2003/04 season in two knock-out competitions, the **Carling Cup** and in particular, the **FA Cup**. In the latter, the Reds reached the final for the first time since winning The Treble in 1999. Here's a reminder of the matches they won on the way to Cardiff…

FA Cup

Third Round

United felt a strong sense of déjà vu when the third round draw was made. For the second time in three years, the Reds were required to start their FA Cup campaign away to Aston Villa. And just like the meeting in January 2002, it was the home team that scored first in January 2004. Gareth Barry's goal in the 17th minute left United trailing until midway through the second half. Fortunately, Fergie had a couple of aces up his sleeve in Ruud van Nistelrooy and Roy Keane. The striker and skipper came on ten minutes into the second half; soon after this, the tie was turned on its head by two Paul Scholes' goals. Great substitutions, Sir Alex!

Fourth Round

United's next tie was, for many people, what the FA Cup is all about, the coming together of giants and minnows, the chance for David to beat Goliath. Northampton Town were dreaming of a shock result at their Sixfields Stadium when, in the fourth minute, their goalkeeper Lee Harper saved Diego Forlan's penalty. But although United were made to wait another half an hour before they finally put one past Harper, they were too strong for the Third Division side. Van Nistelrooy, Giggs and Keane were not on the United team-sheet, but Silvestre, Forlan (eventually) and Hargreaves (o.g.) were all on the score-sheet.

Fifth Round

After their fourth round visit to a lower league ground, United were back where they belong in the fifth round with a home tie against very familiar opposition. Manchester City were the Valentine's Day visitors to Old Trafford in a derby packed full of goals and other incidents. So packed, in fact, we've put the details on another page of this annual (see page 54). All you need to know here is that the Reds romped through 4–2!

Sixth Round

Fulham were hoping lightning would strike twice when they made their second trip of the season to Old Trafford, four months after pulling off a shock 3–1 win in the Premiership. And just for a minute, the fans inside the famous stadium were wondering if it might happen again. Literally a minute, because that it was all it took for Ruud van Nistelrooy to equalise in front of the East

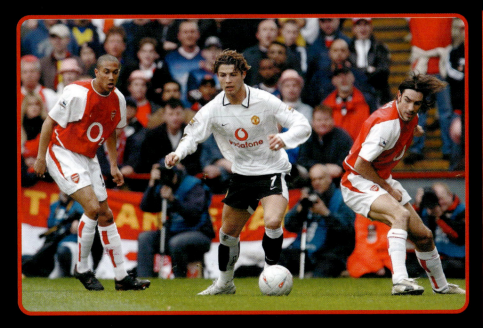

Ronaldo keeps the ball away from Arsenal's Clichy (left) and Pires.

Road to Cardiff

Aston Villa 1–2 Man Utd
04-01-2004
Scholes 2

Northampton 0–3 Man Utd
25-01-2004
Silvestre, Hargreaves (own goal), Forlan

Man Utd 4–2 Man City
14-02-2004
Scholes 2, Van Nistelrooy, Ronaldo

Man Utd 2–1 Fulham
06-03-2004
Van Nistelrooy 2

Arsenal 0–1 Man Utd
03-04-2004
Scholes

Stand after Steed Malbranque had buried a 23rd minute penalty at the Stretford End. It took Ruud a bit longer to get the crucial second goal – it came in the 62nd minute from Ronaldo's cross, not long after the Portuguese star had hit the bar with a free-kick.

Semi-final

If the critics thought United's cup run would hit the buffers against the Premiership leaders Arsenal, they were made to think again when Scholes scored first in the semi-final at Villa Park. Going a goal down was a rare and therefore serious test for the treble-chasers from North London, and with their star-man Thierry Henry starting on the bench, they found it difficult to get back into the game. In fact, Arsenal found it impossible to bounce back against Roy Carroll and Wes Brown, who both performed brilliantly for United in the positions usually occupied by Tim Howard (rested) and Rio Ferdinand (suspended). Keane, Scholes and Fletcher won their midfield battle with Vieira, Edu and Pires, and Ronaldo mesmerised his markers. It was arguably United's best team performance of the season, just when they needed it. Next stop, Cardiff!

Carling Cup

Third Round
Leeds 2–3 Man Utd 28-10-2003

United's Carling Cup game at Leeds gave players like Nicky Butt and David Bellion the chance to stake a claim for more regular first-team football. From the Academy, Kieran Richardson started on the left wing, while Chris Eagles and Eddie Johnson came on as subs for their senior debuts. All played their part in a pulsating cup tie which went into extra-time and would have gone to penalties, had Eric Djemba-Djemba not won the match with an outrageous looping shot in the 117th minute!
Final score, 3–2 to the Reds.

Fourth Round
West Brom 2–0 Man Utd 03-12-2003

Albion were flying high in the First Division so there was little surprise when, after only six minutes, Haas brought the house down at The Hawthorns with a superb volleyed goal past Roy Carroll. The goalkeeper had one moment of glory when he saved Koumas' penalty, but he couldn't stop Dobie from doubling West Brom's lead just after half-time. No more goals were scored, so United's short Carling Cup run was over.

Kings of

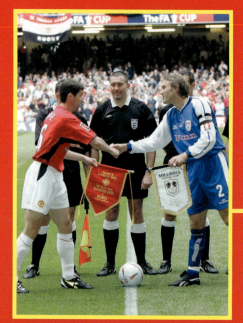

Manchester United ended the 2003/04 season on a high when they beat Millwall 3–0 at the **Millennium Stadium in Cardiff**. The result brought the Reds their fifth FA Cup triumph under Sir Alex Ferguson and the eleventh in their glorious history, confirming them as the undisputed **Kings of the Cup…**

Sir Alex Ferguson

"The scenes at the end of the match epitomised what the romance of the Cup is all about. There is a special relationship between the players and the fans. It's marvellous that our efforts during the season have been rewarded with a trophy. I feel proud of everybody attached to the club."

the Cup!

Ruud van Nistelrooy
"I had missed the last penalty I took but I was convinced I would score this one. That's why I gave it full power and it was good to see it go in. The FA Cup is the biggest cup competition in the world and to play in a final, and win it, is a fantastic feeling."

Roy Keane
"It's always nice to win a trophy, and the latest is always the nicest. Ronaldo's goal just before half-time was important because Millwall were gaining in confidence. We just had to be patient and professional."

Tim Howard
"To get a medal and a cup in my first year is awesome. I can't say anything else about it. I didn't have a lot to do but what we did, we did well, so we'll take the win!"

Gary Neville
"Ruud, Ryan and particularly Ronaldo produced some really good moments for us. I think Ronaldo can be a world-class player, right up with the very top players in the world."

Ryan Giggs
"It was a great day for the fans, it is a great place for them to watch football and we were able to give our supporters the result they wanted. Ronaldo's goal capped off a great display. Every time he touched the ball he did some damage, he was a constant thorn in Millwall's side. He really excites the crowd, and he excites the other players."

Cristiano Ronaldo
"It's great to win my first trophy with United. I have already achieved a lot of things but I still want more. To win the League is my number one objective. It is a big compliment that my manager and team-mates say so many good things about me. I hope to repay them by playing more good games and helping the team to achieve our goals."

Fergie's Team Sheet

United v Millwall

FA Cup Final, 22 May 2004

14. Howard
2. Neville
6. Brown
27. Silvestre
22. O'Shea
7. Ronaldo
16. Keane
24. Fletcher
11. Giggs
18. Scholes
10. van Nistelrooy

Subs: 13. Roy Carroll (Howard, 84), 3. Phil Neville, 8. Nicky Butt (Fletcher, 84), 19. Eric Djemba-Djemba, 20. Ole Gunnar Solskjaer (Ronaldo, 84)
Goals: Ronaldo 44, Ruud 65 pen, 81

FRANCE

Mikael Silvestre – Defender
Born: 9 August 1977, Chambray-Les-Tours

Mikael Silvestre wasn't the first French player to join Manchester United – but he was the second to be transferred to Old Trafford from an Italian club! The defender arrived from Inter Milan early in the 1999/2000 season and shared his debut with goalkeeper Massimo Taibi, who had also made the switch from Italy to England just a few weeks before him. Mikael has learned to speak English very well during his five years in Manchester – in fact, he even sends text messages in English! But not only is Mikael bi-lingual, he's also bi-positional! In other words, he can play in two different positions, left-back and more often now at centre-back, where he developed a strong partnership with Rio Ferdinand 2003/04. This has helped Silvestre's international career with France – hopefully he'll be one of their key players at the next World Cup, when it's played in Germany in 2006.

Have United played there?

Yes – quite a few times in European competitions, including five UEFA Champions League matches in the last six years. The Reds won in Bordeaux and returned home with draws from Lille, Nantes and Monaco. They have lost only once in France in recent years, 0–1 to Marseille in October 1999.

Did you know?

Mikael's former club, Auxerre, have had the same manager, Guy Roux, for more than 40 years! Like Fergie, Roux is renowned for bringing young players through into his first team. Eric Cantona is just one example!

Louis, David and Goofy open the Manchester United Soccer School at Disneyland, Paris.

David Bellion – Forward
Born: 27 November 1982, Paris

Like Silvestre, David Bellion also blossomed in a foreign country before coming to United. He was only 18 when he moved from Cannes – the French beach resort where a famous film festival is held every year – to Sunderland which is also on the coast, but not quite as glamorous! David's time in North East England was well worth it, however, because it brought him to the attention of Sir Alex Ferguson. The Boss signed the speedy striker in the summer of 2003, just in time to go on the pre-season tour of America. His very first appearance in a red shirt was in Seattle, USA, where he scored in the 4–0 friendly win against Celtic… bravo, Monsieur Bellion! The next time he netted for United, he was in a very different setting again – Leeds in West Yorkshire, in a Carling Cup match at Elland Road. Although his first-team appearances were limited in his first season, Bellion's future looks very bright – hopefully as bright as two other boys who started their career in Cannes, Patrick Vieira and Zinedine Zidane.

Did you know?
David's birthplace, Sevres, is a swanky town on the outskirts of Paris. Gustav Eiffel, the man who designed and give his name to the world-famous Eiffel Tower, used to live there.

Louis Saha – Forward
Born: 8 August 1978, Paris

Louis Saha needed just 18 minutes in his Manchester United career to score his first goal for the club. But even that was slow by his standards! In his very first appearance at Old Trafford for Fulham (in 2001/02), he hit the net in the 4th minute, much to the surprise of the home fans and United's French goalkeeper, Fabien Barthez. And although Saha scored again early in the second half, the afternoon really belonged to Ruud van Nistelrooy. It was Ruud's Premiership debut too and he celebrated with two goals and an impressive 3–2 win to the Reds. If the two were rivals then, they are now a deadly duo. In fact, they both scored on Saha's United debut, another 3–2 win, this time against Southampton. United are actually Saha's third English club. The year before he joined Fulham, he played for Newcastle on loan. He scored two goals in eleven games for the Magpies before returning to Metz in North-East France.

Did you know?
Louis' first club, Metz, finished second in the French League in 1998. It's the only top-two finish they have achieved since the league was formed in 1933!

Rest of the World United

How would the Reds line up if Fergie could only pick players from outside the UK?

1. **Tim Howard** (USA)
2. **Eric Djemba-Djemba** (Cameroon)
3. **Quinton Fortune** (South Africa)
4. **Mikael Silvestre** (France)
5. **John O'Shea** (Ireland)
6. **Roy Keane** (Ireland)
7. **Cristiano Ronaldo** (Portugal)
8. **Kleberson** (Brazil)
9. **Louis Saha** (France)
10. **Ruud Van Nistelrooy** (Holland)
11. **Ole Gunnar Solskjaer** (Norway)

Goal # 1: August 12, 2001
Liverpool 2–1 Manchester United
FA Community Shield
Ruud's first century for United started at the Millennium Stadium, Cardiff. As Premiership Champions, Van Nistelrooy's new team competed for the Community Shield with the FA Cup winners Liverpool. It wasn't to be United's day, but there was still a special moment for Ruud in the 51st minute. He rounded off a flowing team move with a clinical finish past his fellow Dutchman, Liverpool keeper Sander Westerveld.

Football is very much a team game. But there are times in a team game when you have to salute the talents of an individual, especially a world-class player like Ruud Van Nistelrooy. Here we raise a toast to Ruud's first century of goals for United, highlighting his milestone strikes en route from 1 to 100…

Goal # 50: November 23, 2002
United 5–3 Newcastle United
FA Premiership
The 50th minute of this entertaining match had only just passed when Ruud scored his 50th goal for the Reds. It was also his third on the day, giving him the second hat-trick of his United career. And not only that, it came at a crucial time in the game, just one minute after Alan Shearer's thunderous free-kick had pulled Newcastle back to 3–2 down. It was a milestone goal for Shearer – his 100th league goal for Newcastle.

Goal # 10: November 20, 2001
Bayern Munich 1–1 United
UEFA Champions League
Like his first goal, Ruud's tenth was also scored away from Old Trafford against one of the club's biggest rivals. This time, it was United's great European foes Bayern Munich who were punished by Ruud's prowess. Both teams ended up going through to the quarter-finals but neither of them reached the final – despite Van Nistelrooy scoring a total of eight goals in the campaign, including one in the semi-final against Bayer Leverkusen.

Goal # 25: January 29, 2002
Bolton Wanderers 0–4 United
FA Premiership
Ruud clocked up his quarter-century in a local derby at the Reebok Stadium. His 25th United goal in the 84th minute ensured that, margin-wise, it was United's biggest away win of the season (they later scored 5 at West Ham but conceded 3). However, the Dutchman would not dispute that Ole Gunnar Solskjaer was the real hero of the evening – Ruud's strike partner scored United's first three goals on a great night for the Reds.

Goal # 100: February 7, 2004
Everton 3–4 Manchester United
FA Premiership
Ruud reached his century in another high-scoring match. Even the Everton fans thought Ruud's 100th goal, plus another two in the first-half from Louis Saha, would be enough to give United an easy win. However, the Blues bounced back in wintry conditions after the break to draw level at 3–3. The Reds were getting ready to kick themselves – hard – until the 89th minute when Ruud headed in the winner, his 101st goal for United!

European

United's European adventure in 2003/04 was much shorter than we expected. But even though it ended after just eight games, there were still some enjoyable evenings for us to savour, both at home and abroad…

Panathinaikos

Away Destination:
Apostolos Nikolaidis Stadium, Athens, Greece

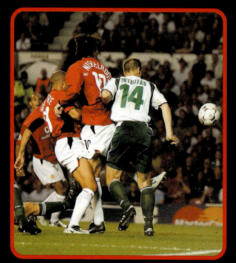

Silvestre scores the first of five!

Ironically, the Reds produced their best European result in their first match of the campaign as Panathinaikos were pulverised 5–0 at Old Trafford. Some of the names on the score-sheet were unfamiliar – Giggs didn't score and neither did Van Nistelrooy, even though both started and finished the match in attack. Instead defender Mikael Silvestre and several midfielders scored the goals.

One of them, Eric Djemba-Djemba, fired in his first goal for United in the 83rd minute. Eric's first was United's fifth and had been a long time in coming… they'd been 4–0 up at half-time!

The away trip to Panathinaikos was played more than two months later, by which time United were looking good to go through. It was the last-but-one game in Group E but there was still time for things to go wrong if the Reds weren't careful. Fortunately, they were careful and, when it counted, clinical. Diego Forlan scored in the 85th minute to make the final score 1–0 to United. The Reds were going through to face Porto in the knock-out stages, Panathinaikos were going out.

VfB Stuttgart

Away Destination:
Gottlieb-Daimler Stadium, Stuttgart, Germany

The venue and team were new to United – in fact, new to the Champions League. VfB Stuttgart stunned their experienced opponents with two superb goals in the space of two minutes, early in the second half. They needed to be special shots to beat Tim Howard. The American goalkeeper was in great form as he later proved by saving a penalty from Fernando Meira. Ruud van Nistelrooy pulled a goal back

for United with another penalty, after Ronaldo had been pulled down by the Stuttgart goalkeeper, but it wasn't enough. The Germans won 2–1.

Back in Manchester, it was a different story. Both teams were already through to the second round so the only things at stake were pride and pole position in the group. United claimed both, beating Stuttgart 2–0 with goals by Giggs and Van Nistelrooy. Ruud's header on the brink of half-time made him the club's joint all-time top scorer in Europe – level on 28 with Denis Law.

Rangers

Away Destination:
Ibrox Stadium, Glasgow, Scotland

The prospect of playing Rangers got everyone excited when UEFA made the group stage draw for 2003/04. The media called it the Battle of Britain, a clash between the champions of England and Scotland. But most important, it was an opportunity for United to take six points and stamp their authority on Group E. They did this, but by the narrowest of margins north of the border. The atmosphere at Ibrox was electric – at least until Phil Neville silenced the home fans with an early goal. The early goal was the only goal and so United flew home with half the job done.

The other half of the job was easier

Ruud scores against Rangers.

to complete on home soil. Again, United scored early – through Forlan – but this time they trebled their tally with Ruud scoring just before and fifteen minutes after the break. The Battle of Britain brought four goals and six points for United but left the men from Ibrox empty-handed.

FC Porto

Away Destination:
Estadio do Dragao, Oporto, Portugal

Familiar opponents, unfamiliar ground, unexpected result. That was the story of United's trip to Portugal, where they faced the

team they had beaten so emphatically in March 1997. FC Porto were at a brand new stadium for United's visit in February 2004, the Estadio do Dragao. Unwittingly, the Reds gave their opponents a house-warming present by playing poorly and enabling Porto to take a shock 2–1 lead into the second leg. Only South Africans scored in the first leg; Benni McCarthy netted twice for the home side, after Quinton Fortune, his international team-mate, had opened the scoring for United.

Fortune's away goal was supposed to give United the edge in a two-legged tie. And so it did… for an hour! Paul Scholes headed the Reds in front in the 32nd minute and even though he had a second goal unfairly disallowed for offside, United looked good to go through on the away goals rule. But then Porto were awarded a dangerous free-kick in the 89th minute. In came the ball… and out it went, from the normally safe hands of Howard to the waiting boots of Costinha. He scored and Old Trafford fell silent with astonishment. Final score: 1–1, 2–3 on aggregate. The European adventure was over for another season!

The World of UNITED
EUROPEAN STARS

Netherlands

Ruud van Nistelrooy – Forward
Born: 1 July 1976, Oss

The Netherlands has produced some of the greatest players, clubs and national teams that Europe or even the world has ever seen. The Netherlands team of the Seventies finished World Cup runners-up in 1974 and 1978. Their number one superstar was Johan Cruyff, a skilful playmaker whose son Jordi played for United a few years ago. The next great Netherlands side won the European Championships in 1988 with players like Frank Rijkaard, Ruud Gullit and the goal-scoring machine that Ruud Van Nistelrooy is often compared with – Marco van Basten. Now Ruud is trying to help Holland recapture their past form and glory in the 2000s, alongside players such as Chelsea star Arjen Robben and Fulham goalkeeper Edwin van der Sar. But whatever happens to the Netherlands as a national team, clubs like PSV Eindhoven and Ajax will surely continue to produce top quality players... let's hope some of them follow Ruud to Old Trafford!

Have United played there?

Oh yes! Their most memorable match in the Netherlands was played in the port of Rotterdam in 1991 when Fergie won his first European trophy as United manager, the Cup Winners Cup. The Reds beat Barcelona 2–1 in the final, despite one or two of the opposition players having the advantage of playing on familiar soil – the Spanish club's scorer on the night, Ronald Koeman, is Dutch! United have more recently played against Feyenoord and PSV Eindhoven in the group stages of the UEFA Champions League.

Did you know?

Ruud is quite a common name in Dutch football history. The great team of the 1970s featured a legendary player called Ruud Krol, and the 1988 European Champions included Ruud Gullit who later went on to manage Newcastle and Chelsea in the English Premiership.

Norway

Ole Gunnar Solskjaer – Forward
Born: 26 February 1973, Kristiansund

Ole Gunnar Solskjaer became only the second Norwegian to play in the Premiership for Manchester United when he came on as a substitute and scored against Blackburn Rovers on 25 August 1996. United's first player to come from Norway was Ronny Johnsen. He made his first appearance

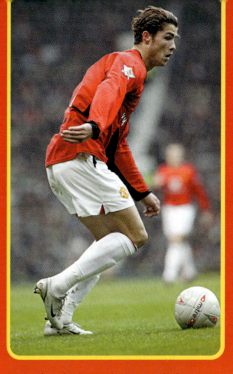

still flying the flag, thrilling thousands of fans back home who support one club or the other. Maybe you could try lip-reading when Solskjaer and Riise next play against each other on TV… you might learn a new language!

Have United played there?

Yes. Every so often, United pay a visit to Norway to acknowledge the fantastic support they receive over there. The last time they played in Norway was on their pre-season tour of Scandinavia in July 1998. Solskjaer scored one of the goals in the 2–2 draw with Valerenga; Denis Irwin grabbed a hat-trick (including two penalties) in the 4–0 thrashing of SK Brann.

Did you know?

Ole Gunnar has scored more than a century of goals for United. He scored his 100th goal on the first day of the 2002/03 season, at home to West Bromwich Albion. Typically, it wasn't just an important goal for Ole Gunnar, it was a crucial one for the team, turning a disappointing draw (0–0) into a wonderful win (1–0)!

the week before Ole Gunnar did, away to Wimbledon, a game best remembered for David Beckham's goal from the halfway line! At the time, there were quite a few Norwegian names in England. For example, Lars Bohinen and Henning Berg, who both played for Blackburn on Ole Gunnar's debut. In more recent years, the number of Norwegians in the Premiership has decreased, but Ole Gunnar and Liverpool defender John Arne Riise are

Portugal

Cristiano Ronaldo – Winger
Born: 5 February 1985, Madeira

Cristiano Ronaldo didn't take long to make an impact as United's first-ever Portuguese player. His dazzling debut in the 4–0 win over Bolton Wanderers had journalists and fans buzzing with excitement – and he only played for half an hour! Some of the hype had a lot to do with the number on his back – seven – that had previously been worn by David Beckham, of course. But although Ronaldo can take great free-kicks and corners, he's different from David in the way he can dribble around opponents with tricks and skills like the step-over. Ronaldo comes from a country well known for its fancy football. Real Madrid star Luis Figo and 1960s legend Eusebio are just two of the Portuguese players who rank among the greatest footballers of all time. In time, Ronaldo hopes to join them in the hall of fame and win trophies with his country and with his club, Manchester United. There's much more to come from the Madeiran marvel!

Have United played there?

Yes – Portugal's top clubs have crossed swords with United in the past, with the Reds usually having the upper hand. In the 1968 European Cup Final, they beat Eusebio's club Benfica 4–1 at Wembley, and in 1997, they thrashed Porto 4–0 in the UEFA Champions League quarter-final. However, Porto gained their revenge in 2004 when they scored a late goal at Old Trafford to knock United out of European football's biggest competition.

Did you know?

United players urged Fergie to sign Ronaldo after he'd played against them in a pre-season friendly in Portugal in July 2003. The young star ran the Reds ragged, helping Sporting Lisbon to beat them 3–1.

Famous Namesakes

Can you match the Manchester United stars with their famous namesakes? There are 15 celebrities listed here from the worlds of music, movies, TV and sport but their first names or surnames are missing. Your challenge is to fill in the blanks with the first names of the 15 United stars in our photo-grid.

_____ **McCormack**, actor, star of TV comedy *Will & Grace*

_____ **Henman**, tennis player, Britain's number one

_____ **Rhodes**, TV chef, supports Man United

_____ **Mickelson**, golfer, won the 2004 US Masters

Meg _____, actress, starred in *Kate & Leopold* and *You've Got Mail*

_____ **Makaay**, footballer, plays for the same international team as Van Nistelrooy

_____ **Snipes**, actor, starred in *Blade*

_____ **Rhys-Davies**, actor, played Gimli in *The Lord of the Rings*

_____ **Maradona**, footballer, won the World Cup in 1986

_____ **Campbell**, athlete, won the 200m silver medal at the 2000 Olympic Games

_____ **Parks**, pop star, 2003 winner of BBC talent show *Fame Academy*

_____ **Neeson**, actor, played Qui-Gon Jinn in *Star Wars Episode I: The Phantom Menace*

Craig _____, pop star, hit songs include *Walking Away* and *Re-Rewind*

Sean _____, pop star, had a hit with Beyonce in 2003 called *Baby Boy*

_____ **Armstrong**, musician, famous for an old jazz song called *What A Wonderful World*

Answers on page 60.

THE AMERICAS

Brazil

Kleberson – Midfield
Born: 17 June 1979, Urai

Fergie's search for a Brazilian star took him first to the French club Paris St Germain in the summer of 2003. Sadly, Ronaldinho said "no" to United and joined Barcelona instead. Fortunately Fergie still had a Brazilian ace up his sleeve, in the form of Ronaldinho's international team-mate Kleberson…

Have United played there?

Yes – the Reds played in Brazil for the first time in their history in January 2000. They were taking part in the first FIFA Club World Championship, a bit like a mini-World Cup for clubs. United played three games at one of the most famous stadiums in the world, the Maracana Stadium in Rio de Janeiro. Unfortunately, they managed only one win – against South Melbourne of Australia. A draw with Necaxa of Mexico and a defeat by local Brazilian team Vasco Da Gama meant United failed to reach the final.

United have also played against a Brazilian club in Japan. They beat Palmeiras 1–0 in Tokyo to win the 1999 Inter-Continental Cup Final – an annual match between the champions of Europe and South America.

Did you know?

Kleberson is only the fifth World Cup winner to play for United. The others are Sir Bobby Charlton and Nobby Stiles (England 1966), Laurent Blanc and Fabien Barthez (France 1998). Only Charlton and Stiles were United players at the time of winning the World Cup; the other three joined the Reds afterwards.

Uruguay

Diego Forlan – Forward
Born: 19 May 1979, Montevideo

Diego Forlan scored one of the best goals of the 2002 World Cup in a thrilling 3–3 draw with the African underdogs from Senegal.

Unfortunately, Diego's glorious shot came too late to win the match for his national team, Uruguay, and like the favourites, France, they bowed out in the first round.

Have United played there?

No – but Liverpool FC play there every week! Not United's arch-rivals, of course, but a Uruguayan club with the same name. They're based in the capital city of Uruguay, Montevideo, and have a stadium with a capacity of 9,000… nearly as big as Anfield where Liverpool FC in England play! (Only joking…)

Did you know?

Uruguay won the first-ever World Cup in 1930. The tournament was held in Uruguay and only 13 teams entered but even so, it's a proud statistic for Diego's home country. They beat Argentina 4–2 in the final.

USA

Tim Howard – Goalkeeper
Born: 3 June 1979, North Brunswick, NJ

Tim Howard has finally solved one of the biggest problems that Sir Alex Ferguson has ever had to deal with at Manchester United – how to successfully replace the legendary goalkeeper Peter Schmeichel, who left a big hole when he quit United in 1999. Several great keepers, including Fabien Barthez, tried their best to fill it, but it wasn't until Howard arrived that the shadow of Schmeichel really begin to disappear…

Howard's physical presence and command of the penalty area made United even more difficult to beat during his first season at the club. His agility also made the men playing in front of him feel more confident. As Wes Brown said in a TV interview, "Even if you make a mistake, Tim will probably save it. When you've got someone like him behind you, it gives

One to Watch

Jonathan Spector – Defender
Born: 3 January 1986, USA
United signed three players from the USA in 2003 – Tim Howard from New Jersey Metrostars, striker Kenny Cooper from Solar SC in Dallas and Jonathan Spector from Chicago Sockers. The promising defender has plenty of time to develop his skills and to learn from senior players like Rio Ferdinand and Gary Neville. Maybe one day he could help his fellow American, Mr Howard, to keep clean sheets for the first team!

the back four and the rest of the team more confidence."

Have United played there?

Yes – Tim Howard made his first appearance for United on their USA Tour 2003. Tim played in the 4–1 win against Juventus in the Giants Stadium, New Jersey. The Reds played and won three other matches in Seattle (against Celtic), Los Angeles (Club America) and Philadelphia (Barcelona). The pre-season tour was so successful that United returned to the USA in 2004.

Did you know?

Tim Howard wasn't the first goalkeeper from the USA to play for Fergie. Paul Rachubka, born in California, beat Tim to it by three years when he played in the FIFA Club World Championships in 2000, as a sub against South Melbourne. Rachubka was only 18 at the time, having risen through the youth team ranks at United. He signed for Charlton Athletic in May 2002.

Rio Ferdinand and the Mystery of the Missing Shirt

1 Manchester United are on their pre-season tour of the USA and everything seems perfect. The sky is blue, the sun is shining…

2 And there are United fans everywhere, wanting to meet and greet their heroes.

3 The players are in good spirits…

Tim: "I love this country, man!"

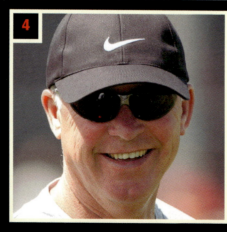

4 And so is the manager.

Fergie: "Keep running, lads – only 10 more laps of the field to do! You need to burn off all those American burgers and French fries!"

5 But wait, what's this? Rio Ferdinand seems a bit down in the dumps.

40

Rio: "I can't believe it… my United shirt's gone missing!"

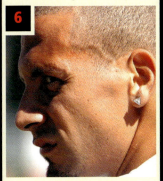

Rio: "The rules in America are really strict. If I can't find my shirt, I won't be able to play in the match on Saturday."

Although not all of them take the search seriously…
Roy: "Hey, Rio. Isn't that it, on your head?"

The next day, while the rest of the boys prepare for the big match…

Fergie: "Mike, you'd better organise a search party. I really need Rio to play on Saturday, so we need to find that shirt… and fast!"

Mike: "Yes, boss. Right away, boss."

Rio: "Huh? Oh. Yeah, yeah, very funny, Roy."

Rio tries his hand at an American sport…

Rio: "Hey, this is cool. I wonder if Ryan and Ronaldo can dribble a ball like this… Watch me!"

The players hunt high…

Roy: "Ha, ha, ha. Sorry, Rio. I was only teasing. No need to get shirty with me. Ha, ha, ha. Get it? No need to get shirty!"

Rio enjoys basketball so much, he plays until it's almost dark. And then, as he leaves the court, he begins to think about his future…

Rio: "Maybe it was fate, losing my football shirt. I think it's time for a change of career. I'll speak to the gaffer as soon as I get back to the team hotel."

And low…

Despite a massive search, Rio's shirt doesn't show up. Sir Alex Ferguson breaks the bad news to the media…

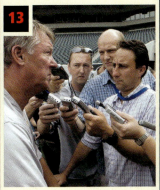

Fergie: "It's a ridiculous situation, but the soccer authorities over here won't allow Rio to play without his proper match shirt. It's a real blow for the boy."

After chatting with Rio, the manager calls a press conference for the morning, when he makes a shock announcement…

Fergie: "Rio Ferdinand is here to say farewell. He's off to join the Chicago Bulls basketball team!"

OR IS HE?! Find out what happens next to Rio Ferdinand, Sir Alex Ferguson and Manchester United by logging on to ManUtd.com!*

*You won't find this story on ManUtd.com, reader… only true stories!

2004/05 Track

O ne of the targets that Sir Alex Ferguson sets his team every season is to improve on the previous campaign. With this fill-in chart, you can keep track of when the United players reach various landmarks in the 2004/05 season, and compare them with their 2003/04 achievements.

FA Premiership	Season 2004/05	Season 2003/04
First Home Win		Home Match # 1: Bolton Wanderers 4–0
First Away Win		Away Match # 1: Newcastle United 2–1
First Home Draw		Home Match # 3: Arsenal 0–0
First Away Draw		Away Match # 13: Fulham 1–1
First Home Defeat		Home Match # 5: Fulham 1–3
First Away Defeat		Away Match # 2: Southampton 0–1

Domestic Cups	Season 2004/05	Season 2003/04
FA Cup – Progress		Winners (beat Millwall 3–0 in the final)
Carling Cup – Progress		Round # 4: West Bromwich Albion 0–2
Community Shield		Winners (Beat Arsenal 4–3 on penalties; 1–1)

UEFA Champions League	Season 2004/05	Season 2003/04
Progress		Last Sixteen: FC Porto 2–3 (on aggregate)
First Home Win		Home Match # 1: Panathinaikos 5–0
First Away Win		Away Match # 2: Rangers 1–0
First Home Draw		Home Match # 4: FC Porto 1–1
First Away Draw		No Away Matches Drawn
First Home Defeat		No Home Matches Lost
First Away Defeat		Away Match # 1: VfB Stuttgart 1–2

Record

Goals	Season 2004/05	Season 2003/04
First Premiership Goal		Ryan Giggs v Bolton (Premiership Match # 1)
First Premiership Clean Sheet		Tim Howard v Bolton (Home Match # 1)
First FA Cup Goal		Paul Scholes v Aston Villa (Round # 3)
First FA Cup Clean Sheet		Roy Carroll v Northampton Town (Round # 4)
First Carling Cup Goal		David Bellion v Leeds United (Round # 3)
First Carling Cup Clean Sheet		No Clean Sheets in Carling Cup
First Champions League Goal		Mikael Silvestre v Panathinaikos (UCL Match # 1)
First Champions League Clean Sheet		Tim Howard v Panathinaikos (UCL Match # 1)

Debuts	Season 2004/05	Season 2003/04
First New Arrival		Tim Howard v Arsenal (Community Shield)
First Academy Player		Chris Eagles v Leeds United (Carling Cup Rnd # 3)

Discipline	Season 2004/05	Season 2003/04
First Yellow Card		Phil Neville v Arsenal (Community Shield)
First Red Card		Darren Fletcher v Middlesbrough (Match # 28)

Cameroon

Eric Djemba-Djemba – Midfield
Born: 4 May 1981, Douala

Fergie's first player from Cameroon came to Manchester via France. The battling young midfielder started his career with Nantes, helping them to win the French league championship in his first full season 2000/01. The next season saw Eric win the African Nations Cup with Cameroon, but lose to United in the UEFA Champions League with Nantes. Despite the scoreline (the Reds won 5–1), the young African must have done something to catch Sir Alex's eye because, just over a year later, the United boss signed him.

Have United played there?

Not yet, but maybe Eric could persuade United to go on a tour of his homeland? They would have plenty of teams to play against, especially in Douala where Eric was born. There are six clubs there, all with Douala in their name: Dynamo, Dragon, Caiman, Leopards, Union and Oryx Douala. Sounds confusing!

Did you know?

Eric is hoping to follow in the footsteps of Cameroon legend Roger Milla and play for his country in the World Cup Finals. Milla still holds the record for being the oldest goalscorer in World Cup history; he scored against Russia in the 1994 tournament at the grand old age of 42! However, he really made his name by scoring four goals in the 1990 World Cup. Cameroon almost knocked England out in the quarter-finals; they were leading 2–1 with ten minutes to go before England rallied to win 3–2.

South Africa

Quinton Fortune – Defence/Midfield
Born: 21 May 1977, Cape Town

Like Eric Djemba-Djemba, Quinton didn't take the direct route from Africa to Manchester. He was signed in August 1999 from a Spanish club, Atletico Madrid. Before that, he'd played for Tottenham in England – but only as a youth player. Fortune's first few seasons at

China

**Dong Fangzhuo – Forward
Born: 23 January 1985, Dalian**

United provisionally signed Dong Fangzhuo, their first Chinese player, in January 2004. He had previously impressed the Reds when he was on trial from his club in China, Dalian Shide. Sir Alex Ferguson said, "We brought him over for a month and we liked the look of him. He's aggressive and quick." Dong himself said about the trial, "I learned such a lot. My positioning and running into the box became sharper and my heading definitely improved." Dong's transfer from Dalian Shide was only provisional because UK work permit rules meant he couldn't play for the Reds straightaway. First, he had to gain experience with United's partner club in Belgium, Royal Antwerp, where he linked up with fellow young Reds players Eddie Johnson, Arthur Gomez and Phil Bardsley.

Have United played there?
Yes. The Reds played in China itself for the first time on 21 July 1999, winning 2–0 in a pre-season friendly against Shanghai Shenhua FC. On the same tour, they played in Hong Kong, beating South China FC 2–0. United also beat South China 1–0 on their previous summer tour of Asia, in 1997.

Did you know?
Dong's former club, Dalian Shide, were not formed until 1994. They won the Chinese league for the first time in 2000.

United saw him flit in and out of the first team; he wasn't helped by his international call-ups for South Africa at awkward times of the season! To be fair to Fortune, he's a patriotic guy and playing for your country is considered to be the ultimate honour in football. Quinton can also boast the honour and achievement of scoring a goal in the World Cup; in the 2002 tournament he slotted a penalty past Paraguay.

Have United played there?
Yes, they played two games in Johannesburg in the summer of 1993, against Kaiser Chiefs (1–1) and fellow tourists Arsenal (0–2). And not only did they play football, they also met some very important people, including Nelson Mandela!

Did you know?
Quinton was born in Cape Town on the very same day that United won the 1977 FA Cup Final!

Puzzle

Djemba-Djemba Jigsaw

United's ace midfielder Eric Djemba-Djemba is a cool and confident character on the pitch. But in this puzzle, he's gone to pieces! Can you put him back together again?

Come on, you can do it!

A	B	C	D
E 2	F	G	H
I	J	K	L 11
M	N	O	P
Q	R	S	T 17
U 19	V	W	X

Instructions

There are 24 numbered jigsaw pieces above. All you have to do is decide how the jigsaw pieces should be rearranged, using the grid we've provided. Four of the jigsaw pieces have been placed in the grid to start you off. Write a list of the jigsaw piece numbers from 1 to 24 on a piece of paper, and then write the letter of a grid-square next to each one... when you've done it, check your answers on page 60.

46

Time

A Wheel of Fortune

You can make lots of words using the letters in **Quinton Fortune's** name. We'd like you to find 25 – Quinton's squad number – using the clues below, which are either similar or associated words. Good luck!

Three letters
Sprint
Single
Entertainment
Athletic
Hotel

Four letters
Melody
Three
Castle
Worry
Ripped

Five letters
Fish
Vegetable
Almost
Frequently
Mammal

Six letters
Individual
Bad
Idea
Aim
Outlook

Seven letters
Attendance
Exercise
Five
Fire
Wealth

Ruud Words

How many Ruud words can you find in the grid below? We've hidden **20 words** that are associated with **Manchester United's** brilliant goal-scorer. Happy hunting… the solution can be found on page 60.

R	E	C	O	R	D	D	H	K	U	H
E	U	V	E	D	R	H	E	C	N	N
R	E	U	H	N	E	E	I	I	I	N
O	S	I	D	A	K	E	N	R	S	I
C	T	V	S	L	I	R	D	T	T	U
S	D	N	A	L	R	E	H	T	E	N
L	V	S	P	O	T	N	O	A	L	I
A	S	A	Y	H	S	V	V	H	R	T
O	N	I	N	E	T	E	E	N	O	E
G	O	R	A	N	G	E	N	T	O	D
I	R	Y	R	U	T	N	E	C	Y	S
D	U	T	C	H	E	N	T	E	N	E

net
PSV
record
Eindhoven
United
Oss
hat-trick
Ruud
nineteen
Van

Heerenveen
Nistelrooy
Dutch
Holland
Netherlands
orange
century
goalscorer
striker
ten

Fergie's
Team Talk

Sir Alex Ferguson loves to talk football, and especially to sing the praises of his talented team at Manchester United. Recently we found a Minidisc on which the manager describes 12 of his players,* but he didn't mention any of their names. Can you work out whom he was talking about?

*11 of the 12 were United players in 2003/04. The other is Liam Miller.

The answers are on page 60.

1 "He's been improving every year since he joined us and has shown great character to come back from his various injury problems. He's doing really well now and we look forward to him making a great contribution to the team in the next few years."

2 "Although he has played wide right as well, we see him as a central midfielder, without question. We have played him on the right so far as it allows him more protection while he's still physically growing. His new contract is in keeping with the tradition at this club of bringing young players through to the first team squad."

3 "He has wonderful balance, loves to attack people's legs and is a fantastic crosser, but we need to be careful with him. At the moment he is like a moth to the light: playing in the Premiership before big crowds, he wants to do his tricks all the time. What we're trying to do is make him more effective but it will take time and we mustn't rush him. We know how to look after our young players here and given time he will only get better and better."

4 "For years he has lived on his raw energy as a player but we couldn't expect him to do that forever and he has adapted brilliantly to become a more mature footballer. His influence on the rest of the team is still immense – as he showed against Rangers and then when we needed to be strong at Anfield. He channels his commitment to good effect these days."

5 "It's a tremendous leap for a player to come straight from his country into the Premiership. I expected him to stand still, even go backwards for a time, but he has taken it in his stride and has been so impressive. He has everything required for his position: his agility, courage and speed figure high among his qualities."

6 "He always assesses what's happening around the field and to have scored more than 100 goals for us is fantastic, especially considering he's spent so much time on the bench. But then it shouldn't be surprising: he studies the game so well and is always at the right edge to come on and make a difference."

7 "He has broken every record since he has been here. His improvement and continual commitment to the club is an asset. He has proved to be a fantastic signing and his contract extension is great news for the club and the fans."

8 "He is a young and exciting talent and has made incredible progress. We have got a young and gifted centre forward – his performances against Manchester United have showed us that. To have finally secured this deal is fantastic and a great boost to the club."

9 "We've been trying to build a young squad of players that will serve us for a few years and he falls into that category. In some ways he's similar to Roy Keane but I see more of Brian McClair in him. He's got a fantastic engine, he sees the space in front of him, he's got the ability to run past opponents from deep positions and he's a good finisher. For a small lad, he's very good in the air."

10 "He is a young, athletic midfield player who can play in a number of positions. One of the reasons we sold Juan Sebastian Veron was because we knew we were getting him. That shows how highly we regard his talent."

11 "We did not know whether he would go abroad or come to us, and we are delighted he has chosen Manchester United. He is a young player with great potential who will fit into the club's future plans very well."

12 "He is a young player we watched throughout the season before we signed him, and he impressed us each time with his understanding of the game. He's quick, aggressive and a good passer of the ball, and is the kind of athletic footballer we had been looking for. He has shown his development playing in a very good international team, and he looks like a Manchester United player in every sense."

Alphabet Quiz

This quiz is different because we give you the answers, all you have to do is match them with the right questions! The 26 answers are the players' names.

David Bellion
Wes Brown
Roy Carroll
Eric Djemba-Djemba
Chris Eagles
Dong Fangzhou
Rio Ferdinand
Darren Fletcher
Diego Forlan
Quinton Fortune
Ryan Giggs
Tim Howard
Roy Keane
Kleberson
Liam Miller
Gary Neville
Phil Neville
John O'Shea
Kieran Richardson
Cristiano Ronaldo
Louis Saha
Paul Scholes
Mikael Silvestre
Ole Gunnar Solskjaer
Mads Timm
Ruud van Nistelrooy

Keep a note of your answers as you go through the alphabet. The process of elimination may help you to crack some of the more difficult questions. **Enjoy!**

The answers are on page 60.

A is for... **Anderlecht.**
Who scored against them in the 2003/04 Champions League?

B is for... **Belgium.**
Who played there on loan during 2003/04?

C is for... **Cannes.**
Who started his football career there?

D is for... **Dudek.**
Who slotted two goals past him at Anfield in 2003/04?

E is for... **Elland Road.**
Who made his debut there in the Carling Cup?

F is for... **France.**
Who played in the league there immediately before joining United?

G is for... **Greece.**
Who scored there for United in the 2003/04 Champions League?

H is for... **Hungary.**
Who earned his first England cap there during 1998/99?

I is for... **Ibrox.**
Who scored the winning goal there for United in October 2003?

J is for... **JJB Stadium.**
Who played his home games there before he signed for United?

K is for... **Kenny.**
Who turned down Kenny Dalglish to join United in the summer of 1993?

L is for... **Lithuania.**
Who scored his first international goal against them during 2003/04?

M is for... **Middlesbrough.**
Who scored against them in the 2003 FA Youth Cup Final?

N is for... **Nottingham.**
Who scored four goals there in February 1999?

O is for... **Odense.**
Who was born there on Hallowe'en 1984?

P is for... **Portsmouth.**
Who scored his first United goal against them?

Q is for... **QPR.**
Whose former club shared their ground in 2003/04?

R is for... **Rennes.**
Who started his career with them in 1995/96?

S is for... **Scotland.**
Who scored a hat-trick against them in 2003/04?

T is for... **Torpedo.**
Who made his debut against Torpedo Moscow in 1992/93?

U is for... **Urai.**
Who was born there in June 1979?

V is for... **Villa Park.**
Who scored three goals there for United in the 2004 FA Cup run?

W is for... **Waterford.**
Who was born there in April 1981?

X is for... **XIV.**
Who wore that squad number for United during the 2003/04 season?

Y is for... **Yorkshire.**
Who played his home games in that county from 2000 to 2002?

Z is for... **Zimbabwe.**
Which player was born nearest to that country?

RED ALERTS

This puzzle tests your memory of United matches and your ability to learn a new language ... text language!

The following **six messages** have been sent from one Reds fan to another on a mobile phone. Each message describes a classic United match from the past five years (1999–2004). In each case, you have to work out the opposition, United's goalscorers and the final score. To help you, we've published one photo from each game on the opposite page. Enjoy! The answers are on page 60.

GR8 RZLT 2DAY. :-)
ALWYZ GD 2 BT SCSRS.
4LAN, YES 4LAN, SCRD 2 GLS.
SCSRS GK HD ABSLT NTMARE!
1ST GL WZ V FNEE! :-D
CD HV BN 2-2 BUT FAB
MD GR8 SVE FRM HMAN.

1

YES!! I CNT BLEV IT!! WVE DN IT!!
THORT W'D BLWN IT. 0-1 @ FT
BUT TS & OGS SCRD INJ TME. :-))
STL CLBR8TNG 1ST GL WEN 2ND
WNT IN! AF SHD BE SR AF AFTR THIS.
TH MN IS A LGND. THY R ALL LGNDS
NW! WHO PT TH BLL IN TH GRMNS NET?
O-G-S!

2

EXLNT GME :-) SHME ABT TH AGG SCR :-
(RNLDO IS JST AMXZNG. HT-TRCK: ALL GR8
GLS. FAB DDNT STND A CHNS. RVN SCRD
FR US, OG + 2 4 BCKS. MAYB BECKS WLL
JN RM IN SMMR? THTS TH RMR IN TH
PPRS. RM SHD WIN UCL NW. DFFRNT
CLSS. JST HPEWE CN WN TH PREM THS
C-SN! GOT 2 CTCH RSNL.

3

WOW! WOT A MTCH! BCKS SCRD IN 1ST HRF. BRKMP EQLSD 2ND HRF. THN REF SNDS KENO OFF! DWN 2 10 MEN. THN 90TH MNIT. P NEV BRNGS DWN RAY PRLR IN BOX! PEN 2 RSNL. SCHM SVS IT! EXTR TME. MTCH GNG 2 PENS UNTL RG GTS BALL OFF VERA, GOS RND DFNCE & SCRS!!! YES!!! BST GL IVE EVR CN! HPE I CN GT TKTS 4 FNL @ WMBLY.

WOT A CMBCK!! THORT WE WRE DED & BR'D @ H-T. THY WRE 3-0 UP. WE WRE SHMBLS @ TH BCK IN 1ST HRF. DNO WOT AF SD 2 PLYRS @ H-T BUT IT OBVSLY WRKD! AC SCRD JST AFTR H-T, THN BLNC MDE IT 2-3. RVN EQLSD. 3 OR 4 MINS L8R JSV SCRD. FNLLY, BCKS SCRS JST B4 TH END! THR FNS CDNT BLV IT. AT H-T THY WR FLL OF IT. THY DSPRRD WHN BCKS GL WNT IN! GR8 JRNY HOME. CDNT STP SNGING! :-o THNK IV LST MY VCE!

UNBLVBLE! 2 BD DFNSS, 7 GR8 GLS, GR8 RZLT IN TH END. SHD HV BN 6-0 UP AT H-T, NO KDDNG. LS & RVN R ON FIRE. 2 GLS ECH. LS 12.8M? BARGN! BUT WOT ABT TH DFNS? 3-0 UP, THN 3-3. GD JB RVN SCRD @ TH END. THY CD HV WN IT 2! T-HO MD GD SVE FRM WN RNNY. UTD R EXLNT IN ATTCK, :-(@ TH BCK. WE MSSD RIO. DNT THNK WLL WN TH LGE THS SSN. RSNL DNT GV GLS AWY LK WE DO!

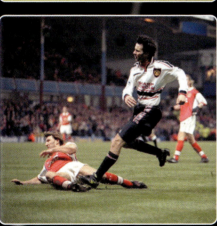

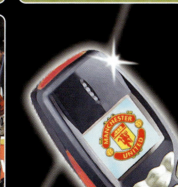

Derby Days

Premiership and European success might have eluded United in 2003/04 but they were still top dogs in Manchester! The Reds played the Blues three times during the season, beating them twice at Old Trafford and scoring loads of goals. They also visited City's new home for the first time…

Kleberson's Derby Debut
13 December 2003

Above: **Kleberson leaps over City midfielder Steve McManaman.**

You'd expect a man who has won the World Cup to have experienced virtually everything in football! But even Kleberson's breath might have been taken away by the pace and passion of his first-ever Manchester Derby. The Brazilian star was in the thick of the action at Old Trafford, helping to set up United's first and final goals. Both were scored by Paul Scholes; the England hero headed in Kleberson's perfect right-wing cross to make the score 3–1 to United in the 74th minute. Points in the bag!

Valentine's Day Derby
14 February 2004

Above: **Gary Neville exchanges angry words with McManaman.**

Most romantic day of the year? Not when there's local pride and progress in the FA Cup at stake! There was certainly no love lost between Gary Neville and Steve McManaman, who squared up again when the United defender felt he was fouled in the penalty area. The referee Jeff Winter didn't give a penalty but he did take action when players piled in from both teams for a brawl! Gary was sent off but United still won the match 4–2, despite playing the entire second half with ten men! Paul Scholes scored two goals again, and was joined on the scoresheet by Ruud and Ronaldo. Tim Howard also had a brilliant game.

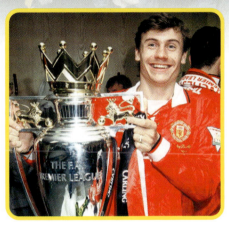

28 years!

Derby Day Nightmare
14 March 2004

Ronaldo battles with City's Shaun Wright-Phillips.

There's an old saying where Derbies are concerned... "The form-book goes out of the window!" In other words, they're impossible to predict and that was certainly true of United's first visit to the City of Manchester Stadium. Nobody could foresee City winning the match 4–1, especially not at half-time. After going 0–2 down, the Reds played brilliantly in the first half. They pulled a goal back, scored yet again by Scholes. Not only that, but Ronaldo hit the crossbar with a superb shot. Sadly, to use another cliché, it was a game of two halves! City turned on the style in the second half and grabbed two more goals to inflict Sir Alex Ferguson's worst defeat in a Manchester Derby since losing 5–1 in 1989!

Andrei won trophies with United, but nothing with City.

Did you know?

Several legends have played for City after winning trophies with United, including Peter Schmeichel, Andrei Kanchelskis and Sammy McIlroy. Denis Law, whom Reds fans called The King in the '60s, joined the Blues in the early '70s. He even scored for City at Old Trafford towards the end of the 1973/74 season, when United were relegated from the top flight. Going back even further, Billy Meredith started his professional career with City in 1894. He then joined United, helping them to win two League Championships and the FA Cup. In 1921 he rejoined City as player-coach and then went back to United again as a coach in 1931!

United fans count the years since City won their last major trophy.

Did you know?

The first Manchster Derby in the Football League was played on 3 November 1894. United, who were then known by their original name Newton Heath, won the match 5–2.

Did you know?

United have in the past played their home games at City's ground. In fact, it happened for the first three seasons after the Second World War when Old Trafford was badly damaged by German bombs. United also called Maine Road "home" when they first started playing midweek European Cup matches in the late 1950s. Old Trafford had been repaired by then, but unlike Maine Road, it didn't have any floodlights!

Fergie's Foreign LEGION

Six foreign players made their **Manchester United** debuts during the 2003/04 season – David Bellion, Eric Djemba-Djemba, Kleberson, Tim Howard, Cristiano Ronaldo and Louis Saha. Test your knowledge of them with this crossword – there are six clues per player. The solution is on page 60.

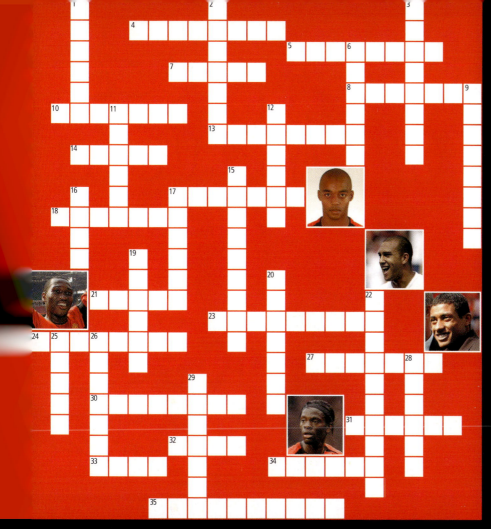

1. Chelsea star who plays for the same country as Djemba-Djemba (6)
2. Team that knocked Djemba-Djemba's country out of the 2004 African Nations Cup (7)
3. Howard's squad number during his first season at United (8)
6. City where Ronaldo played home games before joining United (6)
9. Ronaldo's age when he signed for the Reds (8)
11. Transfer fee that United paid for Ronaldo (to the nearest million) (6)
12. One of Howard's rivals for the USA's goalkeeper position (6)
15. German club that Howard saved a penalty against (9)
16. Black _____ , nickname of David Bellion's previous club (4)
17. French club where Bellion started his career (6)
19. New _____ , American state where Tim Howard was born (6)
20. Month in which Saha signed for United (7)
22. Ronaldo scored his first Premiership goal against them (10)
25. Mike _____ , first referee to book Djemba-Djemba in the Premiership (5)
26. First striker to score past Tim Howard in the Premiership (7)
28. _____ Road, ground where Bellion scored his first competitive goal for the Reds (6)
29. Team-mate who scored two goals in Kleberson's first Manchester Derby (7)

Across

4. Park where Ronaldo set up a last-minute goal for Ruud (8)
5. Tournament that Kleberson won in July 2002 (8)
7. Colour of Djemba-Djemba's home international shirt (5)
8. City where Bellion scored on United's 2003 USA tour (7)
10. Squad number worn by Kleberson during 2003/04 season (7)
13. Other name of Paranaense, Kleberson's previous club (8)
14. Nationality of the team Djemba-Djemba scored his first United goal against (5)
17. Saha missed the FA Cup Final because he was this (7)
18. Ronaldo was born on this island (7)
21. Bellion's birthplace in France (5)

23. _____ Filho, United youth coach who speaks the same language as Kleberson (9)
24. European capital where Saha made his debut for France (8)
27. Saha scored his first goal at Old Trafford past this goalkeeper (7)
30. Nationality of the first Premiership goalkeeper whom Kleberson scored past (8)
31. African city where Djemba-Djemba was born in May 1981 (6)
32. Player who previously wore Saha's shirt number at United (4)
33. Peter _____ , manager who first brought Bellion to England (4)
34. Ruud _____ , Louis Saha's first manager in England (6)
35. Tim Howard's favourite other sport (10)

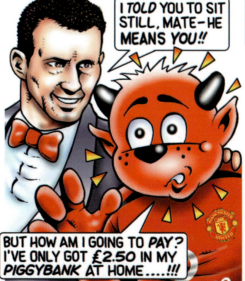

Answers to Puzzles

Famous Namesakes

(Pages 36-37)

Djemba-Djemba: Eric McCormack
Howard: Tim Henman
Neville: Gary Rhodes
Neville: Phil Mickelson
Giggs: Meg Ryan
Keane: Roy Makaay
Brown: Wesley Snipes
O'Shea: John Rhys-Davies
Forlan: Diego Maradona
Fletcher: Darren Campbell
Ferguson: Alex Parks
Miller: Liam Neeson
Bellion: Craig David
Scholes: Sean Paul
Saha: Louis Armstrong

Puzzle Time

(Pages 46-47)

Djemba-Djemba Jigsaw

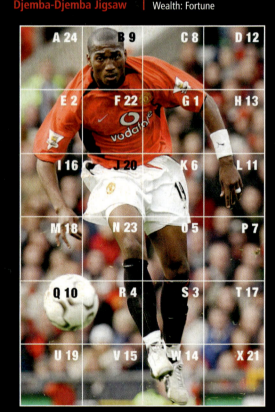

A 24	B 9	C 8	D 12
E 2	F 22	G 1	H 13
I 16	J 20	K 6	L 11
M 18	N 23	O 5	P 7
Q 10	R 4	S 3	T 17
U 19	V 15	W 14	X 21

A Wheel of Fortune

Three letters
Sprint: Run
Single: One
Entertainment: Fun
Athletic: Fit
Hotel: Inn

Four letters
Melody: Tune
Three: Trio
Castle: Fort
Worry: Fret
Ripped: Torn

Five letters
Fish: Trout
Vegetable: Onion
Almost: Quite
Frequently: Often
Mammal: Otter

Six letters
Individual: Unique
Bad: Rotten
Idea: Notion
Aim: Intent
Outlook: Future

Seven letters
Attendance: Turnout
Exercise: Routine
Five: Quintet
Fire: Inferno
Wealth: Fortune

Fergie's Team Talk

(Pages 48-49)

1. Quinton Fortune
2. Darren Fletcher
3. Cristiano Ronaldo
4. Roy Keane
5. Tim Howard
6. Ole Gunnar Solskjaer
7. Ruud van Nistelrooy
8. Louis Saha
9. Liam Miller
10. Kleberson
11. David Bellion
12. Eric Djemba-Djemba

Alphabet Quiz

(Pages 50-51)

A   Liam Miller
B   Dong Fangzhou
C   David Bellion
D   Ryan Giggs
E   Chris Eagles
F   Eric Djemba-Djemba
G   Diego Forlan
H   Wes Brown
I   Phil Neville
J   Roy Carroll
K   Roy Keane
L   Darren Fletcher
M   Kieran Richardson
N   Ole Solskjaer
O   Mads Timm
P   Cristiano Ronaldo
Q   Louis Saha

Ruud Word Search

W   John O'Shea
X   Tim Howard
Y   Rio Ferdinand
Z   Quinton Fortune

R   Mikael Silvestre
S   Ruud van Nistelrooy
T   Gary Neville
U   Kleberson
V   Paul Scholes

Red Alerts

(Pages 52-53)

1. Liverpool 1 United 2 (Premiership 2002/03)
2. United 2 Bayern Munich 1 (Champions League Final 1998/99)
3. United 4 Real Madrid 3 (Champions League 2002/03)
4. United 2 Arsenal 1 (FA Cup Semi-final Replay 1998/99)
5. Everton 3 United 4 (Premiership 2003/04)
6. Tottenham 3 United 5 (Premiership 2001/02)

Crossword: Fergie's Foreign Legion

(Pages 56-57)

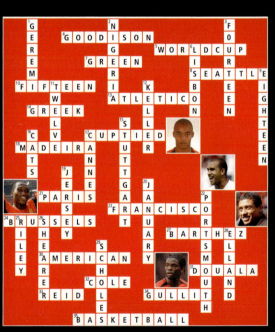

FA Cup Winners